MILLENNIUM BUG

MILLENNIUM BUG

A VW BEETLE SCRAPBOOK

BY KEITH SEUME

BAY
VIEW
BOOKS

FROM

MBI Publishing Company

DEDICATION

This book is dedicated to my dear friend, Ivan Hirst. A more modest man you could not wish to meet.

First published in 1999 by MBI Publishing Company, 729 Prospect Avenue, PO Box 1, Osceola, WI 54020-0001 USA.

MBI Publishing Company books are also available at discounts in bulk quantity for industrial or sales-promotional use. For details write to Special Sales Manager at Motorbooks International Wholesalers & Distributors, 729 Prospect Avenue, PO Box 1, Osceola, WI 54020-0001 USA.

Library of Congress Cataloging-in-Publication Data Available

ISBN 0-7603-0818-7

On the front cover: Bernd Reuters created numerous pieces of Beetle advertising artwork including this happy, sightseeing couple.
On the back cover: Top: VW's New Beetle has launched the Bug craze all over again. *David Newhardt*
Bottom: Owners and aftermarket companies alike have wasted no time in developing tweaks for VW's new icon.

Edited by Mark Hughes

Designed by Bruce Aiken

Printed in Hong Kong

CONTENTS

FOREWORD
BY IVAN HIRST

Keith Seume is a well-established author and writer who has an in-depth knowledge of the Volkswagen and Porsche marques. Packed with facts and detailed information, his books are, nonetheless, readable and amply illustrated.

When he told me he had recently been given free access to the huge store of photographs and archive material at Wolfsburg, I accepted his invitation to read the manuscript of his new book.

Having spent four years at the Volkswagen factory after the war, and followed the company's fortunes since then, I thought had a fair understanding of the cars themselves and associated developments worldwide. But the wealth of his information humbled me—and much of it is published for the first time.

Insofar as the war years are concerned, the author deals only with the cars—such as the Kübelwagen and Schwimmwagen—and tactfully has not delved into the other work with which Porsche and the factory inevitably became involved. Wolfsburg was built to produce cars and, after the aberration of the war, that is what it does today.

I warmly commend this new book to the reader. I have certainly learned much from it.

INTRODUCTION

BY KEITH SEUME

I can still clearly remember the first Beetle I ever saw. It was a red split-window sedan, a Standard model, I think, because I don't recall it having any chrome trim. I used to pass the car every day on my way to school until one day it disappeared, only to be replaced by another split-window—this time a black one. Even though I was only 10 or 11 years old at the time, I found the styling quite irresistible.

Some years later, I got my driver's license and bought a car—an Austin Mini. Why? Well, it was cheap, reliable, and fun. Soon after, I swapped it for a Fiat 600, which was a step in the right direction, as the Fiat was rear-engined and had swing-axle suspension. But I still kept thinking of those two split-windows.

Finally, at the not-so-tender age of 20, I found a 1963 European sunroof model, which had been imported from Switzerland. It was Pearl White with a terracotta brown interior, and I loved it to death.

I soon began to mess with it, modifying the engine as best as I could afford, and spent many hours in the local wrecking yard in search of any spare parts I could afford on my student budget.

One day, as I walked into the yard, I couldn't believe my eyes—there was the red split-window Beetle I had walked by every day on the way to school, some ten years earlier.

I might have bought it there and then, but I didn't because it had already been sold. I couldn't resist taking a closer look and sitting behind the huge steering wheel. It felt as if I was saying goodbye to an old friend.

Now, I can look back at over a quarter of a century of Beetle ownership—I've lost count of how many have passed through my hands, but I think it's something like 30, maybe more—and thank the stars that I walked past that old red split-window on my way to school. Had I not done so, then maybe I wouldn't have decided at such an early age that the Beetle was the car I wanted to own more than any other. Without a Beetle I wouldn't have met so many amazing people or made so many friends along the way.

I hope you enjoy this book—it's my personal celebration of the Beetle. No, it's not full of photos of me and my VWs, but pictures which, I hope, go some way to explaining why I find the Beetle so fascinating. After all, what other car

has been "driven" across the Straits of Messina, or made the star of a series of Hollywood films? How many Fords have you seen dressed up with flowers and turned into a mobile garden?

There may have been over 21 million built, but the Beetle is unique—and so are the people who own them. Now it's the turn of the New Beetle to carry the torch through to the end of the new Millennium. This is one story that is truly without ending…

THANKS

Eckberth von Witzleben and Dr Wiersch at the Stiftung AutoMuseum Volkswagen in Wolfsburg—without access to the official VW archives, this book would not have been possible. Dean Kirsten of *Hot VWs* magazine in the United States for the New Beetle custom and production line photographs. The staff of *VolksWorld* magazine for laying open their files—again! Jacky Morel of *Super VW* magazine for the Super VW Cup and Beetle speedboat photographs. Mark Hughes and Bruce Aiken for their "eleventh hour" production work. My wife Gwynn for her unfailing support in all I do.

Chapter 1
THE PROTOTYPES
From Volksauto to KdF-Wagen...

Although Dr Ferdinand Porsche is popularly credited with dreaming up the idea of a car for the people, in reality there were many others around him who had shared his ideals.

Following the end of World War I, the German economy had been thrown into absolute turmoil. The domestic automotive industry had previously concentrated on producing magnificent coachbuilt vehicles which were designed to appeal to a discerning and affluent clientele. However, with the country drained of its wealth, manufacturers such as Horch and Daimler-Benz found themselves in trouble for the simple reason that there were too few people who could afford to buy their products.

The man in the street could no more dream of owning a car like this than he could of walking on the moon. For him the alternatives were a cheap (and generally unreliable) motorcycle or a horse-drawn cart—or public transport if he was fortunate enough to live in the city.

After spells of working with companies such as Lohner and Austro-Daimler, Porsche had set

The first VW30 prototype is wheeled out of the Porsche workshop in Stuttgart. This was the first of a series of 30 examples, the construction of which was funded by the Deutsche Arbeitsfront, or German Labor Front.

up a design studio of his own at Stuttgart. This allowed him to work unhindered by the pressures previously imposed on him by a large car manufacturer.

Towards the end of 1931, he gave thought to the concept of a small, mass-produced car that would fall into the price range of a typical German worker. He had already tired of designing large, luxury cars and looked forward to a new challenge—one that would be of far more benefit to the German people than yet another limousine.

To Porsche's way of thinking, the conventional mechanical layout of a front-mounted engine driving the rear wheels seemed wasteful in terms of space and manufacturing costs. He preferred the idea of a rear-mounted engine, thus freeing the passenger space of any driveline. The chassis could be lighter and more compact, while the adoption of torsion bars as a

suspension medium meant that further space could be saved and ride quality greatly improved.

This latter point was important, for most small cars, with conventional cart-style springs, were notorious for giving a very rough ride, especially when lightly laden. Torsion bars, on the other hand, act as 'rising rate' springs—the more you twist them, the stiffer they become, but unloaded they remain relatively soft.

Porsche's first design for a "Volksauto" (People's Car) was given the title Project No 12. However, of the manufacturers with whom he discussed the design, only Dr Fritz Neumeyer of the Zündapp motorcycle company showed any interest, for he had also been thinking along the same lines as Porsche.

Three prototypes were built. They featured, at Neumeyer's insistence, a rear-mounted water-cooled radial engine, in preference to Porsche's favored three-cylinder, air-cooled design. As a consequence, they proved to be disastrously unreliable and Zündapp lost interest when the production costs began to spiral.

In the latter part of 1932, Porsche met with the NSU factory and the outcome of their discussions was a new design, Project No 32. Three more prototypes of this new "Volksauto" were built, two with bodies by Reutter, the third by Drauz.

Powered by four-cylinder, air-cooled engines,the NSUs showed a great deal of promise. However, the project came to a premature halt once again when the Italian manufacturer FIAT reminded NSU of a contract, under the terms of which they had agreed not to build cars.

In 1933, an ambitious politician by the name of Adolf Hitler was appointed Chancellor of Germany. He, too, shared an enthusiasm for the introduction of a People's Car and, at the 1933 Berlin Motor Show, announced that he was offering his full support to the German automotive industry, not only encouraging them to build small, inexpensive cars, but also by constructing a network of "autobahns" across Germany on which they could be driven.

In May 1934, Porsche traveled to Berlin to meet Hitler and it was at this meeting that the Chancellor spoke in more detail of his dreams for a "Volksauto". The discussion excited Porsche, except for one thing: price. Hitler was adamant that such a car had to be sold for the price of a motorcycle, and talked of a projected cost of just 1000 Reichmarks—approximately $400 at the time!

Porsche thought this price quite unrealistic but rose to the challenge for he realized that, finally, he had the opportunity to fulfil his ambition to build a car for the people. The first task was to construct some prototypes to present his ideas to the Reichsverband der Deutsche Automobilindustrie (RDA—the German Automobile Industry Association) which had been put in charge of the project.

The first prototypes were given the titles V1 and V2, the letter "V" being short for *Versuch*, or "experimental". The V1 was a small sedan with an aluminum body over a wooden frame. The chassis took the form of a central backbone with a rear-mounted, air-cooled engine and torsion-bar suspension (no surprises there!).

The V2 followed a similar pattern with the exception that it was a convertible, with a crude folding top—at first sight, the inclusion of a convertible in the test program seems slightly strange, for the project was more concerned with providing cheap transport, not with building fun machines to drive on sunny days.

One possibility is that Porsche ordered the V2 to be built so that he could enjoy the experience of driving a "soft-top" while out on test—it makes sense, for the V2 appeared in many photographs in the company of Ferdinand Porsche, having been updated at various times to keep abreast of the latest design changes.

The RDA was pleased with these initial designs and gave the go-ahead to build a further line of prototypes, the V3 series. These were slightly different in that they had an all-steel floor (the V1 and V2 had wooden floor sections) but were otherwise similar to the previous prototypes of the People's Car.

Three examples of the V3 were built and handed over to the RDA for extensive testing—altogether, they covered some 500 miles each day—and proved to be fairly reliable. The RDA was impressed and expressed a desire for the construction of a new series of prototypes, the VW30 range.

A total of 30 cars were built, funded now by the Deutsche Arbeitsfront (DAF—German Labor Front), 29 of which were constructed by the Daimler-Benz company under Porsche's direction. The cars were subjected to an intensive test program, which saw them cover over 1,300,000 kilometers (or more than 800,000 miles!) in all conditions and with varying degrees of success.

Some suffered mechanical failures, others were plagued with punctures (road conditions were often terrible in prewar Germany) and a number of the vehicles were involved in accidents. However, on balance, the VW30s proved to be an enormous success.

In February 1938, Hitler announced at the Berlin Motor Show that his "Volkswagen" (as it was now popularly referred to) was progressing well and that finished vehicles would be ready

soon. Learning from his experiences with the VW30, Porsche ordered the construction of three new prototypes, called the VW303. These proved satisfactory, so a new series of 44 cars was built, these being known as the VW38.

These latest prototypes were true forerunners of the world-beating Beetle, with the familiar rounded lines, a two-piece "split" rear window, and separate running boards, all of which were features of the first postwar models. Compared with other prewar cars from other manufacturers with less funding (let us not forget that Porsche was in the enviable position of having state funding for his ventures), the VW38 was a revelation. Well-made, beautifully designed, and comparatively well-equipped, it was the taste of things to come.

Powered by a 985cc air-cooled, flat-four engine, the VW38 (and its immediate successor, the VW39) had a four-speed transmission and, naturally, torsion-bar suspension, all clothed in an attractive beetle-like body. It weighed a total of 750 kilograms, some 100 kilograms more than originally planned, but was still capable of reaching a cruising speed of 100 kilometers per hour (approximately 62 miles per hour).

By now, the design of the Beetle had been almost finalized—only the matter of how to put it into production remained. Hitler ordered the acquisition of land at Fallersleben, owned by Count von Schulenburg, where a factory would be built.

It was at the cornerstone-laying ceremony at this new factory that Hitler surprised everybody by referring to his new People's Car as the KdF-Wagen ("Strength Through Joy Car"), after the Nazi KdF movement, the purpose of which had been to instill a sense of purpose in the down-trodden German people, by organizing holidays, providing low-cost housing, and, of course, inexpensive motoring.

But whether it was known as a "KdF-wagen", a "Volksauto" or a "Volkswagen", to millions of owners in years to come it would always be a Beetle—a friend who could be relied on when the going got tough.

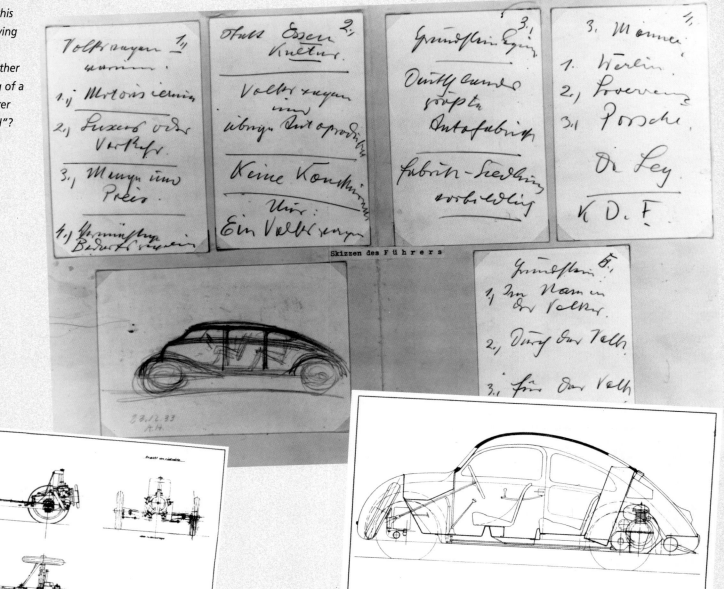

◀ Attributed to Adolf Hitler, this 1933 sketch and the accompanying notes lay down guidelines for a People's Car. It's debatable whether Hitler really did do this drawing of a Beetle-like car—would the Führer really have simply signed it "AH"?

▲ Porsche's designs for Zündapp included this intriguing spine-framed chassis with rear-mounted, five-cylinder, radial, air-cooled engine. Transverse leaf springs provide the suspension at both front and rear. Porsche appeared fascinated by radial engines.

▶ Dated April 27, 1934, this drawing shows one of Porsche's many attempts at designing a People's Car. Already there are distinct similarities between this early design and the Beetle in its final form—note the roof-line and the shape of the side windows.

▲ Another design, this time drawn by Karl Frölich on June 1, 1934, shows a Beetle-like vehicle powered by what appears to be a small two-stroke engine with integral transmission. Rear-mounted gas tank is the main departure from later layouts.

▲ One of the many unsuccessful engine designs for the People's Car—a two-cylinder, horizontally-opposed, sleeve-valve two-stroke. Porsche liked the idea of two-stroke motors because of their low manufacturing cost and light weight.

▲ The one surviving Type 32 now resides in the Volkswagen museum at Wolfsburg. This rare under-body view clearly shows the swing-axle rear suspension and air-cooled flat-four motor. Note the one-piece gearbox casing.

▼ Porsche design No 32 was this vehicle built for Zündapp. Three examples were completed, two featuring bodywork by Drauz, of which this is one. Drauz used artificial leather over a wooden frame—the third example used an all-steel body.

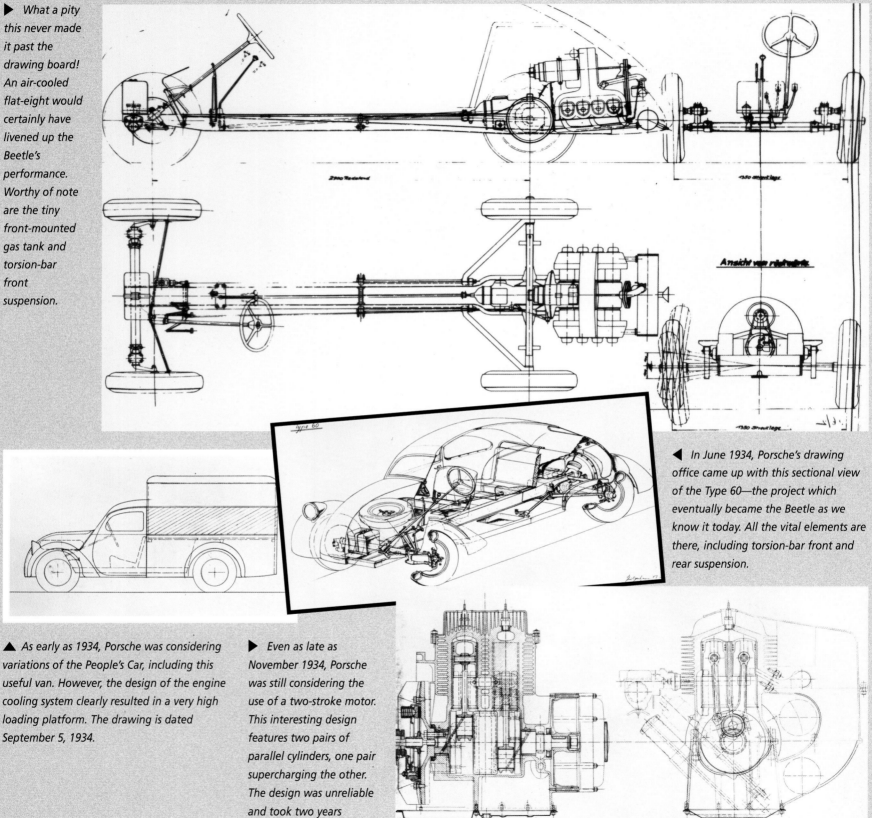

▶ What a pity this never made it past the drawing board! An air-cooled flat-eight would certainly have livened up the Beetle's performance. Worthy of note are the tiny front-mounted gas tank and torsion-bar front suspension.

◀ In June 1934, Porsche's drawing office came up with this sectional view of the Type 60—the project which eventually became the Beetle as we know it today. All the vital elements are there, including torsion-bar front and rear suspension.

▲ As early as 1934, Porsche was considering variations of the People's Car, including this useful van. However, the design of the engine cooling system clearly resulted in a very high loading platform. The drawing is dated September 5, 1934.

▶ Even as late as November 1934, Porsche was still considering the use of a two-stroke motor. This interesting design features two pairs of parallel cylinders, one pair supercharging the other. The design was unreliable and took two years to perfect.

◀ The V1 (sedan) and V2 (convertible) prototypes—the "V" being short for *versuch*, meaning experimental—were built in 1935 using a spine-type chassis. The V1 seen here looks very modern compared with the Dixi alongside.

▼ The "V-series" prototypes were assembled in Porsche's own tiny workshop, with some machine work sub-contracted to local companies. Conditions were far from perfect but a total of five "V-series" cars were built here.

◀ Three V3 sedans were built, two of which can be seen here undergoing testing by the Reichsverband der Deutschen Automobilindustrie (RDA). Tests involved driving each car for a total of 48,000 kilometers over all kinds of roads.

▲ The V2 convertible was quite a pretty little automobile in its own way. Initially, the headlamps were mounted centrally but later, in 1937, the V2 was updated by moving the headlamps to the fenders and fitting chromed bumpers.

13

▶ This photograph of the chassis of the V1 clearly shows the torsion-bar front suspension so beloved by Porsche. Note there are no floorpans: a wooden floor— or steel in the case of the V3— would be added at a later stage.

◀ A previously unseen photograph of a V3 prototype casually parked in the street. The presence of such unusual vehicles created much interest among the public, but test drivers were sworn to secrecy about the entire project.

▲ The rear of the chassis is interesting in that the engine and transmission are suspended from two "forks". The upper cross-member acted as a mounting point for the rear lever-arm shock absorbers (not fitted here).

▲ There's certainly not much room for luggage here! The V1's front compartment was filled with a spare wheel and the gas tank. Note the centrally-mounted headlamps and the screw fittings to secure the hood.

▲ An early wooden model of the VW30 shows how similar the basic design was to that of the V3. The most obvious differences from this angle are the headlamp fairings and the swage lines in the roof. Doors were rear-hinged, "suicide" fashion.

◄ Unusual view of a sectioned VW30 bodyshell shows how it was constructed. Quite why this cut-away was produced isn't clear—perhaps it was done to give high-ranking visitors an inside view of the latest prototype.

► The chassis of the 1937 VW30, with its steel floorpans, bore a far closer resemblance to that of the later Beetle design. Seats could be tilted forwards to gain access to the rear seating. Note the small-diameter bolt pattern of the wheels.

▼ Herbert Kaes, nephew of Ferdinand Porsche and one of the principal test drivers, leans casually against a VW30. Bodyshells are lined up in the background prior to their installation on completed chassis inside the workshops.

◄ The symmetrical layout of the VW30's dashboard suggested that, even at this early stage, a right-hand-drive version was possibly under consideration. Central binnacle houses switches for lights and windshield wipers, along with ignition key and warning lights.

▶ Out on road test, the VW30s attracted enormous interest from passers-by—on this occasion even the test drivers seemed quite happy for people to take a close look. We wonder how many realized the significance of this beetle-like family sedan.

◀ Up in the Alps, Herbert Kaes looks back at "his" VW30 at a rest stop during the rigorous test program. The two-tone color scheme is intriguing—this was a time when little attention was paid to cosmetics.

◀ Kaes spares a few minutes to pose with two young ladies in the snow-covered Alps. Kaes was a born comedian and took every opportunity to have his photo taken, frequently dressed in some humorous outfit.

▼ Life wasn't all rosy, though. The test route took in some of the most extreme conditions imaginable in Europe. The ice-packed underside of this VW30 gives a fair idea of what the test drivers had to contend with.

▲ From the rear, the lack of a conventional window is all too apparent. The view out through the louvers was poor and must have caused problems when backing up. These early prototypes made their contemporary rivals look positively antique.

▶ Access to the front compartment was restricted and many drivers complained about skinning their knuckles when trying to remove the spare wheel. There were few automobiles on the streets back then—and even fewer people.

◀ At the end of each day, drivers were required to complete a detailed test log to record the performance of each prototype. Despite constant hard driving, the VW30s stood up well to the rigors of testing.

▼ It was inevitable that such a lengthy test program would result in some vehicles being involved in accidents. This VW30 was heavily rolled but the roof survived surprisingly intact. One can imagine the driver had some explaining to do!

◀ The completion of the test program was indeed a cause for celebration. Here a presentation is made to one of the test team to mark the end of a successful program. Few other automobiles in history have ever been tested so comprehensively.

▲ Wooden mock-up of the VW38 was built by Reutter, the coachbuilding concern. It was used to assess the overall styling of the new prototypes. Contemporary photographs prove that at least two such mock-ups were built.

▶ Ferry (left) and Ferdinand Porsche compare the new VW38 with its immediate predecessor, the VW30, seen behind them. This latest prototype looked far more modern. Note its excellent paint finish.

◀ A lone VW38 sits outside the gates of Porsche's workshops in Stuttgart. Though much of the technical development of this version was carried out there, the main assembly was largely executed at the nearby Reutter plant.

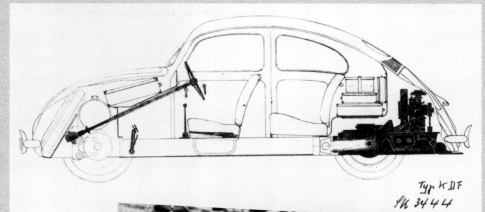

Typ KDF
SK 3444

▲ At the cornerstone-laying ceremony in May 1938, Adolf Hitler referred to the Volkswagen as the KdF-Wagen for the first time in public. This drawing, dated March 1939, also bears the legend "Type KdF" rather than the usual Type 60 designation.

▲ This drawing, first dated 1939 but subsequently revised in 1940, shows the finer details of the KdF-Wagen engine, the design of which remained largely unchanged until 1961. It was truly a masterpiece of engineering.

▲ One of a series of three prototypes (known in some circles as the VW303) displayed at the cornerstone-laying ceremony on May 26, 1938. Hitler is sitting in the rear seat of the cabriolet, while Ferdinand Porsche looks on.

◀ In August 1939, a group of three VW39s ventured up the Gross Glockner pass in Austria, where their arrival at the summit aroused a great deal of interest. Few people had seen a People's Car up close.

▶ Part of the purpose of the trip up the Gross Glockner pass was to carry out a series of radio broadcasts. To this end, one of the cars was equipped with a radio transmitter and mast, which was erected through the sunroof!

▶ This view through the windshield of one of the VW39s also shows the dashboard layout. The switch at the top operates the semaphore turn signals, while the two other switches control lights and wipers. Note gearshift pattern on the right.

▶ Two VW39s speed along a stretch of empty autobahn during a test session. The outbreak of World War II was just around the corner but that didn't put a stop to the test program. Traffic was almost non-existent on these highways in 1939.

▲ The test drives were not always without incident. This prototype—possibly a VW39—was destroyed in a traffic accident. The bent steering wheel and heavily damaged roof suggest the driver is unlikely to have escaped unhurt.

▶ Not only sedan prototypes were built. This simple pickup (Type 825) was also constructed, using a KdF-Wagen sedan as a base. Note the inspection hatch in the pickup bed, to allow easy access to the engine, and the fender-mounted mirror.

▶ Following a traditional "topping-off" ceremony, the construction workers responsible for building the new KdF-Wagen factory added their own personal touch by hoisting this replica of a KdF-Wagen to the top of the scaffolding.

▶ Dated October 2, 1941, this drawing shows the KdF-Wagen in its finished form—a design that would last relatively unaltered until the end of the century. No other car can boast such an amazing history.

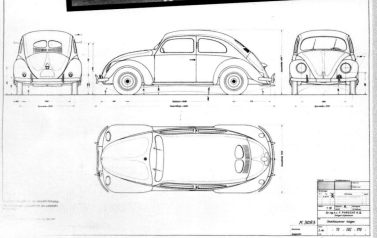

◀ Close-up of the dashboard of a KdF-Wagen—compare this with the photograph shown earlier through the windshield of a similar car. Note the turn signal switch has been rotated through 180 degrees and the windshield wipers park on the opposite side.

◀ In 1939, a group of journalists, including some from abroad, were given the opportunity to drive the KdF-Wagen prototypes. A pause in proceedings allowed them to take in a view of the KdF-Wagen factory construction site.

Chapter 2
PROMOTING A DREAM
How the Beetle was publicized in prewar Germany

There's absolutely no doubt that the prewar publicity campaign set in action by the Kraft durch Freude (KdF) movement to "sell" the Beetle served as a massive propaganda campaign for the Nazi party and all its ideals. The German people, who had long been suffering the effects of an economic depression, were vulnerable to promises of a better life where everyone would share the riches of a new-found wealth, where everyone could enjoy vacations in state-run camps—and where everyone could buy their own car.

Until the KdF dream came along in the 1930s, few people could ever have contemplated ownership of a car. Ever since the end of World War I, the German population had suffered severe deprivations of one kind or another, and cars had come to be playthings of the rich and famous—the poor working class had to make do with small-capacity motorcycles and horse-drawn transport. However, the KdF movement promised equality for all—and it was soon made clear that meant cars for everyone!

It was at the 1933 Berlin Motor Show that Hitler first spoke of a desire to build a

The 1939 Berlin Motor Show marked the official launch of the Beetle (although, at the time, it was known as the KdF-Wagen). Presented on a pedestal decked with flowers, Hitler's People's Car attracted vast interest.

"Volksauto" (People's Car) and his speech sent a shock wave through the German automotive industry, which had previously been more interested in building large luxury automobiles for the monied classes. Few took any real interest in the idea apart from Ferdinand Porsche, who had been working on just such a project with NSU. A year later, at the 1934 Berlin Motor Show, Hitler once again announced his intention to build a People's Car, only this time he was taken a little more seriously by the industry.

By the time the first running prototypes of what was recognizably a Beetle took to the roads, the propaganda campaign was in full swing. There had been many rumors about this new People's Car but few Germans had actually seen one, despite numerous test forays around the Black Forest and up into the Alps. Hitler's favored expression "Volksauto" soon became a

buzz-word for something special, a promise of a better future—and the publicists took full advantage of this new-found sense of hope.

The first proper view the German population had of the new car was when three prototypes were displayed at the official cornerstone-laying ceremony at Wolfsburg in May 1938, although it wasn't until the 1939 Berlin Motor Show that the People's Car was officially launched. At the cornerstone ceremony, Hitler made a passionate speech about his new toy, in the course of which he announced an amazing plan whereby each worker could buy weekly savings stamps until he had sufficient money set by to purchase his own KdF-Wagen.

The scheme proved sufficiently alluring to capture the imagination of some 336,638 people, each of whom spent RM5 every week on a savings stamp. The amount amassed by this scheme was some RM268 million but, alas, not one worker ever took possession of a car, the outbreak of war in September 1939 putting paid to that idea. The plan, however, was magical as far as the KdF movement was concerned, for it provided much-needed capital up front—capital that would help finance the building of the factory and production of the new car. What other manufacturer has ever been in that privileged position? Skeptics have always maintained that this plan was nothing more than a cruel confidence trick, designed to raise funds for the Nazi party. However, after the war, when Nazi accounts were examined in detail, virtually every Reichmark donated to the Sparkarte scheme was accounted for.

No sooner had the savings scheme been announced than the Nazi propaganda machine once more swung into action. Stunningly designed publicity brochures proclaimed the advantages of joining this savings plan and typically formal (almost militaristic) savings cards were printed for distribution among the workers. Today, these Sparkarte cards are much prized by collectors, those filled with stamps being particularly sought after. Inexperienced collectors should be warned, though, that there are some very convincing (but virtually worthless) reproductions in circulation. *Caveat Emptor*!

Accompanying these savings cards were many other extremely collectible artifacts, including slightly crude tin-plate money boxes, the front of which featured a stylized rendition of a KdF-Wagen speeding along a country road. Intended for those who found it hard to buy a RM5 savings stamp in one go, the money box allowed everyone the chance to save for his or her own car as and when finances allowed.

Then there were the board games. Today, every household has a Monopoly or Scrabble game tucked away for those long winter nights when there is nothing on TV but, back in the late 1930s, the game of choice (or so the KdF movement would have you think) was one which showed you how the People's Car was built. A throw of the dice let you take a trip along the assembly lines at the KdF-Wagen factory, with various obstacles in your way to slow down your progress (not that any such problems existed at the real factory, of course!). Instead of the more commonplace colored counters, the game used tiny Beetles to mark each player's progression through the factory.

There were at least two versions of this board game—a second was produced after the war—and both took you through the design and manufacturing process before letting you loose on the roads in your Beetle. Needless to say, any such games are also high on the "wish list" of any collector today, their colorful graphics making them particularly attractive. Interestingly, the original game made use of the VW logo at a time when KdF-Wagen was the official title.

Publicizing the KdF-Wagen took many forms. Throughout Germany, numerous events were held to raise public awareness of the KdF-Wagen, with a traveling show touring the countryside which enabled people in all areas of the Fatherland to take a close look at Hitler's dream project. There was enormous interest shown in the car, with huge crowds gathering every time the show rolled into town. People were invited to come along and examine the car, but no one was actually allowed to drive it. That privilege was reserved for high-ranking military officials and Hitler's own cronies. There were even tombolas which featured Beetles as prizes—although, of course, none was ever won because none was available—and hundreds of star-struck punters handed over their hard-earned Reichmarks in the vain hope of winning. Quite simply, the KdF-Wagen mesmerized the whole of Germany.

Other companies got in on the act, too. Friedrich Volk exhibited an unfinished KdF-Wagen bodyshell at a trade exhibition in Leipzig in March 1939 to publicize the company's machine tooling, which had been used at the Wolfsburg factory. Electrical supplier Robert Bosch also referred to the new car in its publicity. However, perhaps the most outrageous piece of opportunism was by the Ford Motor Company, which capitalized on the widespread public interest in the KdF-Wagen by referring to its "Cologne" model as a "Volkswagen"!

For me, though, the most fascinating prewar publicity material is the series of photographs taken in the apparently carefree days of 1938 and early 1939. They show the KdF-Wagen in the German countryside, frequently in the company of attractive young ladies and dashing young men. Looking at these photographs, it's hard to imagine that a world war was on the horizon, with all the horrors that would entail. It's also difficult to grasp that this was a publicity campaign spear-headed by one of the most evil regimes ever to walk this earth, for the photographs are breathtaking in their innocence.

The cornerstone-laying ceremony, held at Wolfsburg on May 26, 1938, was the first opportunity that most people had to see the People's Car close up. Three prototypes were displayed: a sedan, rag-top (sunroof), and convertible.

▲ In an effort to spread the KdF-Wagen gospel, many high-ranking officials were given the opportunity to drive one of the prototypes, among them Hermann Goering, seen here with Ferdinand Porsche examining a cabriolet.

▶ The only known photograph of Goering actually driving a KdF-Wagen, with Porsche sitting in the back seat. The location is Carinahalle, Goering's country estate. Note the chromed bumpers and "banana" bumper guards fitted to this example.

▶ The original KdF-Wagen brochures were full of evocative imagery which painted a picture of carefree times, with happy families speeding down the autobahns at 100 kilometers per hour in their prized new cars. Who could believe that a world war was about to begin?

Der Innenlenker

◀ In common with most automotive advertising of the era, early brochures suggested the KdF-Wagen was far bigger than it really was. Here, a proud father looks on while his young son stands in awe of the new family car.

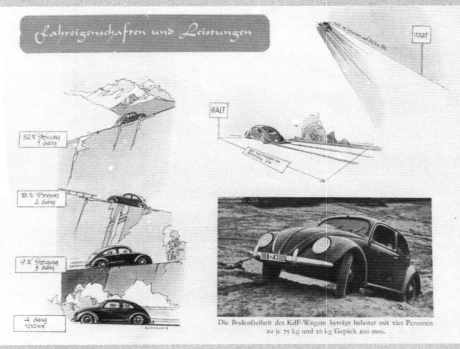

Fahreigenschaften und Leistungen

START

HALT

32.5° Steigung 1. Gang

13.% Steigung 2. Gang

9.% Steigung 3. Gang

4. Gang 100 kg

Die Bodenfreiheit des KdF-Wagens beträgt belastet mit vier Personen zu je 75 kg und 50 kg Gepäck 200 mm.

▲ A bust of Hitler looks down upon a bare KdF-Wagen chassis at the Berlin Motor Show. Foreign journalists were fascinated by the mechanical specification of the KdF-Wagen but, at the time, few took the car seriously.

▶ Brochures were packed with technical information, showing such things as hill-climbing ability in each gear, maximum speed, braking distances, and acceleration times. They even boasted of the KdF-Wagen's ground clearance.

▶ The Sparkarte scheme was very clever, enabling workers to save for their own KdF-Wagen by putting aside money every week. To promote the scheme, this colorful brochure was produced, showing an Alpine scene, complete with speeding Beetle.

▲ This is a money box produced to help less well-off families save for their Sparkarte savings stamps. A counter kept a record of how much money the box contained, while stylized artwork offered inspiration to reluctant savers.

▶ "You must save five marks each week if you wish to drive a KdF-Wagen," suggests this publicity poster for the Sparkarte savings scheme. Little did anyone realize at the time that not one person would ever buy a Beetle under this scheme.

▶ A well-preserved example of a Sparkarte savings card belonging to the author. The document looks for all the world like a military pass rather than a way to save for a dream car. The card was issued in July 1943 to Franz Platzer, a farmer.

▶ Sparkarte stamps were green with a small Beetle embossed in white. The words around the Beetle read "KdF-Wagen—Die Deutsche Arbeitsfront". It took 50 such stamps to fill one book, and five books were needed to pay for the car and insurance.

▶ To while away the days (months? years?) before taking delivery of your KdF-Wagen, you and your family could play this educational board game, which took you on a trip through the factory and out onto the open roads of Germany.

▶ This second, postwar, version of the game featured revised graphics, including a new design for the box lid. The artwork was by Bernd Reuters, the most famous of all Volkswagen publicity artists. The game board was also redesigned in this version.

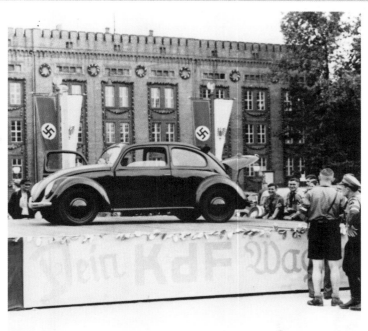

▲ Through 1938 and 1939, travelling displays showed off the new People's Car and gave the German populace a chance to examine it at close quarters. Needless to say, such exhibitions aroused great interest.

AM MONTAGEBAND

▲ "Roll up! Roll up! Buy a ticket and win a Beetle!" If only it had been that easy. Despite the elaborate savings scheme and several prize-draw competitions, no private owner ever came to drive a KdF-Wagen. The outbreak of World War II put paid to that.

▲ Close-up of the game board showing a Beetle passing down the assembly line. Annotation on the "route" shows a pause for tire changing and a road junction, along with a warning about cyclists. Artwork is simply beautiful.

▶ Everyone was keen to exploit the publicity generated by the KdF-Wagen. This advertisement was placed by the company which made the machine tools used to make the body panels. The company's wares were on display at a trade show in Leipzig.

▲ A famous image of Hitler examining a superbly detailed model of a KdF-Wagen presented to him by Ferdinand Porsche. Hitler took every opportunity to be seen with the KdF-Wagen in an effort to promote his dream. Party officials look politely interested.

◀ Even Henry Ford wanted to get in on the act! This advertisement for a Ford Type "Köln" (Cologne) referred to the car as a "Volkswagen". This was such an evocative name that everyone tried to benefit from it.

▶ All kinds of models of the KdF-Wagen began to appear, including this rather attractive bronze example. Although highly stylized (note the unusual treatment of the rear fenders and apron), it's still clearly recognizable as a Beetle.

◀ This perfume bottle looks crude. Hand-painted, it bears the KdF name on the front and a greetings message on its flanks. An early model such as this is very rare and would fetch a high price if offered for sale.

▲ One of a series of
evocative photographs
taken in 1938-39 to
promote the KdF-
Wagen as part of a
whole new way of life.
In the early 1930s,
Germany had been in
the depths of
economic
depression—suddenly
the future looked more rosy.

▲ "He went that a-way!" A series of KdF-Wagen prototypes
featured in several photographs taken around the more
picturesque areas of the German countryside. The contrast
between the old buildings and the "new" Beetle is quite striking.

◄ Picking cherry blossom through the sunroof of a VW39 (KdF-
Wagen prototype), this young lady is obviously happy with life.
Unfortunately, within a year, Germany would be at war with most
of Europe and the KdF-Wagen dream at an end.

▶ This photograph serves to emphasize just how advanced the KdF-Wagen was in design. Until its arrival, the most a German worker could expect to own was a horse-drawn cart or a motorcycle. Few could ever imagine having a car of their own.

▶ "Dad—what happens when I turn this handle?" Family and friends look on cheerily as junior checks out his father's latest acquisition. Sadly, that dream was not to become a reality for several years. Note chrome bumpers but little other brightwork.

▲ The KdF dream promoted healthy living with plenty of fresh air, lots of leisure time and the chance to enjoy your KdF-Wagen to the full. Although the Beetle was a four-seater, three adults, a large dog, and luggage would soon fill it!

▶ *Thanks to the rear-mounted engine, traction on snow-covered roads was far superior to that of more conventional automobiles. Even without snow-chains, this car has no trouble heading for the mountains to enable its occupants to do a little skiing.*

◀ *With three sets of skis strapped to the roof of his car, this guy looks like he's ready for some action with his two girlfriends. Icicles hanging from the bumper and snow under the fenders prove this is no faked studio photograph.*

▲ *Much of the early testing was carried out in the Alps, which also formed a spectacular backdrop for early promotional photos. The air-cooled engine meant that Beetles could climb steep mountain passes without risk of boiling.*

Chapter 3
VW GOES TO WAR
Kübelwagens and Schwimmwagens join forces with the Beetle

Records show that, as far back as 1938, there were plans afoot to build a military version of the Volkswagen. Indeed, the head of the test team responsible for carrying out the road-testing of the VW30 was directed to investigate the development of a military derivative.

The Wehrmacht (German Army) drew up some fairly well-defined guidelines around which a lightweight vehicle should be designed. These included a minimum power output of 25 horsepower, minimum ground clearance of 240 millimeters (around 9.5 inches), and a maximum overall weight of 950 kilograms (2,094 pounds), including 400 kilograms (882 pounds) for men and weaponry.

Porsche accepted the challenge and began to draw up designs based on his current plans for the People's Car. The first tests, carried out in January 1938, involved the use of a regular sedan prototype fitted with balloon tires. Next was a simple chassis with crude angular bodywork and seating for two. This design failed because of a lack of rigidity and inadequate ground clearance. Each of these early military vehicles was largely based on the VW30.

A British Royal Air Force officer, pipe in mouth, climbs out of "his" captured Kübelwagen. Towards the end of hostilities, it was commonplace to commandeer vehicles that had either been captured from the enemy or abandoned by them.

Later, in November 1938, Porsche turned his attentions to the "new" VW38. The end result was the Porsche Type 62, in effect a cut-down sedan which even retained its regular, generously upholstered seating, although it had no doors (canvas flaps were used in their place).

Further Type 62 prototypes were constructed, with purpose-built bodies which offered improved rigidity, but still the problem of ground clearance remained a major stumbling block. In an effort to improve matters, Porsche even tried fitting a third pair of wheels (one on each side alongside the driver and passenger), which were designed to lift the center of the vehicle over any particularly troublesome obstacle. However, even with huge 18-inch diameter wheels fitted, the Type 62 struggled to meet the Wehrmacht's requirements.

The answer was the Type 82, a vehicle similar

in concept to the Type 62 but with the major advantage of massive ground clearance—some 290 millimeters (11.4 inches). This was achieved by the use of reduction gear boxes on the ends of each rear axle and relocated wheel spindles on each front steering assembly.

The reduction boxes not only had the effect of raising the vehicle in relation to the centerline of the rear wheels, but also reduced the overall gear ratio. The Wehrmacht required that any military vehicle of this type be able to drive at walking pace alongside a soldier carrying a back-pack and weaponry. According to the Wehrmacht, this was judged to be 4 kilometers (2.5 miles per hour), a figure impossible to achieve with regular gearing.

Despite its lack of all-wheel drive, the Type 82 soon acquitted itself in testing, "defeating" many rival vehicles in Wehrmacht proving trials. Only the NSU Kettenkrad, a motorcycle half-track, proved its off-road equal, although it couldn't carry the same payload as the Type 82.

This new vehicle went into full-scale production in 1940, despite initial problems with a limited-slip differential unit fitted to aid traction on soft ground. A little ironically, the bodyshells for the Type 82 were produced by an American-owned company, Ambi-Budd, located in Berlin. New bodyshells were sent by rail to Wolfsburg ready to be mated up with completed drivelines.

The Type 82 proved to be one of the most successful military vehicles of World War II and was extremely popular with all who used it. The vehicle came to be known as the "Kübelwagen" (literally translated as "bucket car"—a reference not only to its bucket-like seats but also its overall shape), and saw action in all major campaigns, from the North African desert to the Russian front.

Soon after the Kübelwagen went into action, development began on another military derivative of the KdF-Wagen: the Type 128. This was a four-wheel-drive, amphibious vehicle which was designed to allow soldiers to cross rivers and estuaries without having to rely on a boat.

The first prototype, based on a much-modified Kübelwagen, took to the water in July 1940 and showed sufficient promise to inspire Porsche to develop the concept. It was an ingenious design, with the drive to a front-mounted differential unit being taken from the nose of the gearbox. At the rear of the vehicle, a propeller was driven from the crankshaft.

Under nomal circumstances, the propeller hinged up out of the way but, as soon as it was needed, it could be swung downwards to engage the drive gear. The rear wheels continued to be driven and thus provided a modest contribution to forward progress. Directional control was achieved via the front wheels, which acted as rudders in the water, and were turned by the steering wheel, as normal.

The Type 128 developed into the Type 166, following a meeting with representatives of the Waffen SS who were seeking a lightweight vehicle which could cope with all kinds of terrain, from soft mud to sand, and yet would be small and easy to maintain.

If the Type 128 had any major failing, it was

that it was too big, for it shared the same wheelbase (2,400 millimeters or 94.5 inches) as the Kübelwagen and maneuverability suffered.

Porsche's answer was to produce a new prototype vehicle with a wheelbase of 2,000 millimeters (78.8 inches); this was also 10 kilograms (22 pounds) lighter. Tests showed this to be exactly what the Waffen SS wanted and so the Type 166 "Schwimmwagen" was born.

The Type 166, like the Kübelwagen before it, was another major success and provided both the test team and off-duty soldiers with endless hours of fun, exploring its impressive potential both on land and water.

However, the Kübel- and Schwimmwagens were not the only military vehicles to be developed in the Porsche workshops. There were various somewhat bizarre creations, such as the Type 822 (a Kübelwagen with a large air-raid siren mounted alongside the driver), the Type 155 (a tracked vehicle for use in snow), the Type

157 (a Kübelwagen adapted to run on railroad tracks), and even a dummy armored tank (for use in training).

Two of the most exciting (and practical) vehicles were the Type 82E and the Type 877. The former was a KdF-Wagen bodyshell mounted on a two-wheel-drive Kübelwagen chassis, complete with increased ride height, while the latter was an amazing four-wheel-drive vehicle produced by installing the driveline of the Type 128 Schwimmwagen into a KdF-Wagen. Known as the "Kommandeurwagen", it promised to be an accomplished all-terrain vehicle but suffered handling problems as the front and rear differentials fought against each other on anything other than soft terrain.

In wartime, the Beetle and its derivatives proved to be versatile and amazingly reliable vehicles, winning the admiration of all who drove them. But what else would you expect from a Volkswagen?

A Type 82 Kübelwagen shows off its off-road capabilities in the North African desert. Kübels were held in high regard by all who used them—they were, without doubt, one of the most successful of all military vehicles.

◀ One of the first prototypes built to assess the suitability of the KdF-Wagen as a military vehicle was this crude gun carrier. It consisted of little more than a bare chassis equipped with vestigial fenders. It proved to be too flexible and the idea was abandoned.

▲ This way to the Volkswagen factory! This sign was erected in nearby Fallersleben to direct visitors to the new works where the KdF-Wagen and its derivatives were built. The attractive signpost featured a stylized KdF-Wagen and the silhouette of a policeman.

▲ Nicknamed the "Stuka", but officially titled the Type 62, this was the true forefather of the Kübelwagen. It's seen here in 1939 with an early production Kübel, but was originally built in 1937. The extra pair of wheels was intended to help traction over obstacles.

◀ In mid-1940, the first tests of an amphibious vehicle were carried out. Designated Type 128, it proved to be a success, although it was obvious that much development work would still be necessary before it was "battle-ready".

▲ Clearly, not all testing went to plan! A group of helpers pushes the stricken prototype out of a lake near the Porsche workshops, while an interested group of onlookers watches with some amusement as the troublesome Schwimmwagen is rescued.

◀ Herbert Kaes clearly had great fun showing off the Type 166 Schwimmwagen. Here he demonstrates its impressive off-road capabilities to some serious-looking colleagues. With its four-wheel-drive system, the Type 166 was a very capable machine.

▶ With much of the testing complete, it was time to demonstrate the prototypes to the military. High-ranking army officers gather around an early version of the Schwimmwagen, keen to learn more about this fascinating machine.

▲ Hitler was always interested in how Porsche was progressing and paid regular visits to test sites to view the latest prototypes. Here he examines a Schwimmwagen with Heinrich Himmler (center right), who appears to be hanging on the Führer's every word.

▶ Ferdinand Porsche shows an early Kübelwagen prototype to Hitler. This example was based on a much-modified KdF-Wagen and was considerably more comfortable than the final production version (note the well-upholstered seats).

◀ Several different prototypes were tested before the final Kübelwagen design was chosen. This one is close to the production version but differs in several details, most notably the front fenders. The vehicle's light weight made up for its lack of four-wheel drive.

▶ This photograph shows a works meeting at the new Volkswagen factory, where assembly techniques are being explained to supervisory personnel. In the background, brand new machine tooling is ready to be moved into position.

▶ Both KdF-Wagens and Kübelwagens were assembled alongside each other at Wolfsburg. In the background, a variety of vehicles awaits completion, including a solitary Schwimmwagen and an agricultural tractor!

◀ The Wolfsburg production lines were kept busy through the war. Here, what appear to be chassis for the Type 877 Kommandeurwagen (KdF-Wagen body on Kübelwagen running gear) are assembled prior to having the bodies installed.

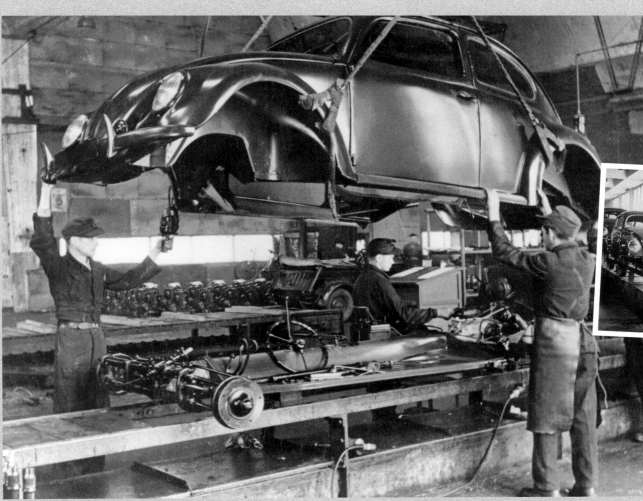

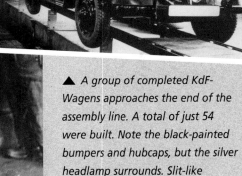

The body of a regular KdF-Wagen is lowered carefully onto a completed chassis. Note the relatively crude finish to the bodyshell and the semi-matt black paint. Thirty years later, Volkswagen continued to use slings under each fender to carry bodies.

▲ A group of completed KdF-Wagens approaches the end of the assembly line. A total of just 54 were built. Note the black-painted bumpers and hubcaps, but the silver headlamp surrounds. Slit-like "black-out" covers are fitted to the headlamps.

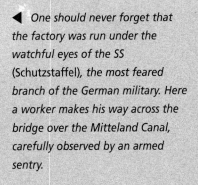

◀ One should never forget that the factory was run under the watchful eyes of the SS (Schutzstaffel), the most feared branch of the German military. Here a worker makes his way across the bridge over the Mitteland Canal, carefully observed by an armed sentry.

▲ Compare this photograph with the earlier one, which showed KdF-wagen chassis being assembled (facing page, bottom right), and it's possible to see that Kübels were built on exactly the same lines as the sedans. Check out the serial numbers on the roof girders for proof!

◀ Much of the workforce consisted of forced foreign labour, housed in atrocious conditions. Three-tiered bunk-beds allowed the SS to cram hundreds of men together in a small space.

▶ The half-track Type 155 was just one of several variations on the Kübelwagen theme. Designed for use in snow and thick mud, it was tested against a half-track motorcycle, the NSU-Kettenkrad. Despite promising results, it never saw production.

◀ Bizarre though this highly-modified Kübel may seem, it had a serious purpose—to help in the training of tank drivers. The dummy bodywork was designed to closely resemble that of a tank, and the driver even had to climb through a hatch to gain entry.

▶ This photograph was taken in 1939, possibly in Berlin. Even though the outbreak of World War II was imminent, there was still time to show off the KdF-Wagen and the new Kübelwagen at trade exhibitions across Germany.

▶ Just over one year into the war, and already there was cause for celebration at the factory as the 1,000th Kübelwagen left the assembly line. Without doubt, the Kübel was one of the most successful vehicles of World War II.

DER 1000. WAGEN
20. DEZEMBER 1940

◀ Because of their ease of construction, Kübelwagens were turned out at an impressive rate. Here a group of them awaits collection and subsequent delivery to their front-line units. How many of this line-up survived the war?

▲ This Schwimmwagen is one of the relatively few survivors and now resides in the United States. Here it's seen at a show alongside a restored P-51 Mustang fighter. Today, Schwimmwagens are among the most highly sought-after of all vintage VWs.

▶ Kübelwagens being repaired out in the field. A complete new chassis sits in the foreground, while mechanics work on replacement engine units. Towards the end of the war, such spares became increasingly scarce.

▲ An American soldier shelters behind a wrecked Schwimmwagen in 1944. The vehicle has been robbed of its wheels and tires—a shortage of rubber in Germany towards the end of the war meant that tires were in huge demand.

▶ In 1945, the factory received a number of direct hits from Allied bombers, which caused a substantial amount of damage. An incomplete Schwimmwagen can be seen suspended from the remains of an overhead production line.

◀ American soldiers in northern France make full use of a "liberated" Kübelwagen while on patrol. The trusty Type 82 soon gained the respect of its former enemies, who grew to appreciate its ease of maintenance and rugged design.

▶ Children claim a Kübelwagen as their own—many military vehicles were abandoned by retreating German troops as the Allied forces pushed towards Berlin. At least a dozen children have managed to squeeze on!

▶ The deprivations of war led to some obscure ideas being tried out, such as this wood-burning conversion of a Type 82E Kommandeur-wagen. Fossil fuels were in short supply, so desperate measures had to be taken to keep the military mobile.

▲ By the time the Allies arrived in Wolfsburg, a lot of the machinery had been removed to dispersal sites in surrounding districts and into the factory cellars, as an air-raid precaution. When discovered, much of this equipment was removed for use "back home", although some was returned to the factory.

▼ This Schwimmwagen was being "road-tested" by British military personnel in the summer of 1945. The propeller could be folded up out of the way when not in use, as can be seen on the lead vehicle. Drive for the propeller was taken from the end of the crankshaft.

▶ The Type 877 was a four-wheel-drive version of the Type 82E, using the Schwimmwagen driveline. This was probably the ultimate development of the KdF-Wagen, but only 667 were built between 1942 and 1944. Drivers reported dreadful on-road manners!

Chapter 4

POSTWAR YEARS
The British come to the rescue

During the final year of the war, the KdF factory was subjected to repeated air raids by Allied bombers. The first major raid took place on April 8, 1944, when an estimated 2,000 bombs rained down on the works in the space of just five minutes. The raid caused a considerable amount of damage, bringing production lines to a temporary halt. To make matters worse, an American bomber crashed onto the factory on April 29, 1944. Things looked bleak.

However, just under a year later, on April 11, 1945, hopes began to rise at Wolfsburg. The end of the war was in sight, as advancing American troops approached the KdF factory. They actually stopped some kilometers short of the works. The almost unbelievable reason was that the town of KdF-Stadt did not even appear on their outdated maps!

News of the arrival of the Allied forces was met with joy by the remaining workers, many of whom, being forced immigrant labor, were living in fear of reprisals from their former employers. The town sent a delegation to find the American troops, a task made perilous by the fact that the surrounding area was swarming with the last

The standard of finish of the first postwar cars left much to be desired, but that was the least of anyone's concerns. At last, a cheap form of transport to replace worn-out Jeeps and light trucks was made available to the forces of occupation.

remnants of SS regiments and hostile Russian troops, the latter holding any German in very low regard. Eventually, contact was made with the Americans and a sense of security descended on the town once more.

Following the full cessation of hostilities in Europe, Germany was divided into four sectors, these being placed under the control of either British, American, French, or Russian military command. None of the other countries took especially great interest in the fact that the KdF factory lay within the British sector—only later did the Russians show a desire to take ownership of the VW works but, by then, it was firmly under the control of the British Army, under the command of Colonel Michael McEvoy.

Prior to the war, McEvoy had busied himself building racing motorcycles under his own name, along with modified Wolseley and Morris cars,

known as "McEvoy Specials". He acquired the rights to sell German Zoller superchargers and subsequently spent a period in Germany, acting as a consultant to Mercedes-Benz. Ironically, as a result of this "German connection", McEvoy even had the chance to ride in one of the new KdF prototypes at the 1938 Berlin Motor Show.

It was McEvoy's idea to put the Volkswagen back into production, making use of whatever equipment and parts had escaped damage during the air raids. The intention was to build Kübelwagens—at no cost to the British taxpayer—which would serve as light transport for the occupying forces, whose own trucks had, by this time, become virtually worn out.

Major Ivan Hirst of the Royal Electrical and Mechanical Engineers (REME), seconded to the Military Government (Control Commission), was given the task of putting this plan into action and a few vehicles were assembled from parts lying amid the ruins of the factory. However, any large-scale production of the Kübelwagen proved to be impossible, as the press tooling at the Ambi-Budd factory in Berlin had been destroyed.

The only alternative (thankfully, as history subsequently proved) was to resume production of the KdF-Wagen. A surviving wartime KdF-Wagen was sent to British Army HQ for assessment. Almost by return, Hirst received an order for some 20,000 cars! In addition, the American, Russian, and French military also expressed an interest in acquiring some for their own use.

Conditions at the factory were quite terrible at the time, with considerable bomb damage to the buildings and a shortage of vital raw materials. Ivan Hirst became an expert at working "deals" with other companies to acquire parts or materials necessary to build the VWs. One such arrangement involved exchanging coal from the nearby town of Braunschweig for power generated by the VW power station! Another saw Hirst arrange to have small parts for carburetors made at the Voigtlander camera factory. Necessity was, as always under such situations, the mother of invention.

Despite the hardships, there was still time for a degree of frivolity—on one occasion, Michael McEvoy came to Hirst with the idea for a racing car based on the Beetle. Hirst was less than impressed with McEvoy's timing, feeling that the company had quite enough on its plate without a diversion such as this. However, McEvoy's enthusiasm led Hirst to consider a two-seat version of the Volkswagen and he drew out some ideas which he passed on to Rudolph Ringel, head of the experimental workshop.

Hirst's design was for a stylish roadster with long, sloping rear bodywork that could be made from a second hood, reversed and fitted behind the cockpit area. Ringel constructed a prototype which was then offered to Colonel Charles Radclyffe, Hirst's chief at Military Government headquarters, for his personal use. The car was fitted with a unique dual-carburetor conversion, consisting of a pair of regular carburetors installed on separate, short inlet manifolds. The result was a slight increase in horsepower but at the expense of a flat spot under acceleration.

The "Radclyffe Roadster", as the car came to be known, saw regular use before being involved in a major accident when Radclyffe's driver slid off the road and struck a steel girder. The resultant damage was so severe that the car required a whole new chassis. Eventually, the roadster simply disappeared—nobody knows its ultimate fate, but it was most probably damaged and then scrapped, as were so many military-owned VWs at this time.

The political climate in western Europe was undergoing a period of change, with the Russians, formerly considered allies, becoming less interested in being part of a united Europe but preferring to close their doors to the outside world. The western Allies' policy towards their zones in Germany was also changing. It seemed likely that the VW factory would not be dismantled upon completion of the Allies' manufacturing requirement—as had been intended in 1945. In short, VW had a future.

Hirst and his superiors thus felt that it was time to appoint a German as head of the Volkswagen factory, and began to interview likely candidates, including Heinz Nordhoff, who had previously worked with Opel. Hirst's original intention had been to appoint someone as second-in-command but he was so impressed with Nordhoff that he recommended the German be put in charge of the factory. Following a further interview with Colonel Radclyffe, Nordhoff was appointed General Director with effect from January 1, 1948.

By the end of 1947, production had reached a massive 2,500 vehicles per month and, despite the less than perfect working conditions, a total of 8,987 cars were built that year. Amazingly, a total of 10,020 had been built in 1946, as opposed to 1,785 in 1945. The car, by now officially called the Volkswagen, clearly had a future: a new General Director, a stable domestic economy, and even, thanks to Dutchman Ben Pon, who purchased six cars towards the end of 1947, its first export order.

The real turning point for Volkswagen came in 1948 when German currency reform took place. This move effectively put money into the pockets of the German public, money which could be spent on consumer goods rather than the necessities of life, such as food and clothing. For many, a car was a first priority—after all, few had been able to afford such a luxury for years.

The Beetle was on its way to becoming a world-beater.

A detachment of French soldiers collects a shipment of Volkswagens from the Wolfsburg factory in 1946. The car proved to be extremely popular with the occupying forces in the immediate postwar years.

▶ *Volkswagenwerk GmbH had been a company under the mantle of the Deutsche Arbeitsfront, a section of the Nazi party. With the arrival of the Allies, the works were temporarily renamed Wolfsburg Motor Works. Note the REME (Royal Electrical and Mechanical Engineers) workshop sign.*

▲ *The factory was in a very poor state when "liberated" by the Allies, having suffered a substantial amount of bomb damage. A group of British Army officers surveys the damage while, on the floor below, can be seen two incomplete Volkswagens.*

▼ *This photograph gives an idea of how busy the production lines were under British leadership. Roof panels were particularly problematic to produce due to the scarcity of sheet metal. In the end, roofs had to be made from two or three pieces welded together.*

▲ *When the British re-established production, almost all aspects of manufacturing were performed in-house, including casting the engine crankcases. Working conditions were far from ideal yet, within a few weeks, a number of vehicles had been completed.*

Much of the workforce comprised local men who, only weeks earlier, had been in the German Army. Most were pleased simply to have some form of employment—and security—in what were still turbulent times.

Although the production lines were automated to a degree, the vast majority of assembly work was carried out by hand. In stark contrast to the final months of the war, tires were apparently no longer in short supply!

Major Ivan Hirst's driver, Kurt Hocke, stands next to one of the test cars outside the Wolfsburg factory. Hocke was actually a German-born American who returned to Germany with Ferdinand Porsche following a visit to Detroit before the war.

One of the drivers feigns misery outside the factory gates. It cannot be overemphasized how difficult conditions were at this time. There was still considerable uncertainty over the factory's future and many workers felt deeply unsettled.

▲ The ruggedness of the Beetle impressed everyone who drove it—despite repeated attempts to break test vehicles! This poor VW (loaded with four officers) has become bogged down and is being towed out of trouble.

◄ Production figures for the Beetle really stepped up in the months after the Allies took control. In 1945, no fewer than 1,785 cars were built, followed by an amazing 10,020 the following year. Here, a line of cars awaits delivery.

▲ This stripped bodyshell bears chalk marks from inspectors who have been examining it for possible weak points. This particular body had obviously received some frontal damage in an accident prior to its return to the factory.

▲ An impressive line-up of vehicles awaiting collection, with the main factory building in the background. There was a shortage of the correct headlamps for a while, necessitating the use of modified Kübelwagen units, as seen here.

▲ Cars were refuelled at this gas station within the factory. The cars shown are covered in frost that has started to thaw in the morning sun. This photo was taken in late fall—possibly 1946.

◄ A British officer about to get behind the wheel of one of a new batch of freshly completed cars, some time in 1946. Despite extensive damage to the factory (which can still be clearly seen), production continued at an impressive rate.

▲ Vehicles that could not be collected direct from the factory were sent by train to their ultimate destination. Just visible in front of the trees to the left is a vast scrapyard of damaged Volkswagens.

▶ Army drivers have never had much of a reputation for careful driving and it wasn't long before wrecked Volkswagens started to return to the factory. Here they were stripped of all useful components, such as engines and electrical items.

◀ Little remained of this Beetle—even the front axle had been torn off the chassis, taking part of the frame-head with it. This car was stripped of every reusable component and what was left sent for scrap.

▲ It appears this pickup was built at the factory, possibly to deliver parts to local bases. It was simply constructed, using flat metal sheet to replace the cut-away bodywork of a regular Beetle sedan. Louvers in the rear quarters supply cooling air to the engine.

▶ The same vehicle, minus its pickup bed sides, hitched to a simple car trailer. It's unclear whether or not this trailer was built at the factory. Note the pickup is based on the raised suspension of a Kübelwagen.

▲ A snapshot photograph of an unknown officer with his Beetle and pet German Shepherd dog. Worthy of note are the glossy finish to the paintwork and the contrasting color of the wheels and bodywork.

▶ Even before the war, a cabriolet Beetle (KdF-Wagen at the time) had always been considered. After the war, the go-ahead was given to build a number of prototypes, this being one of the first. In the background is Schloss Wolfsburg.

◀ The cabriolet prototypes were all based on cut-down sedans, hence they retained the original engine cooling louvers seen here. Later production versions, built by Karmann, did away with these louvers in favor of a slotted engine lid.

▶ A variety of designs for the cabriolet top were tried, including this rather outlandish example with landau irons, which gave the humble Beetle the appearance of a 1930s American convertible. Needless to say, this idea was not adopted.

▶ *Rudolph Ringel was in charge of the experimental workshops at Wolfsburg and was the man responsible for building what became known as the "Radclyffe Roadster". This attractive two-seater, built in 1946, remained a one-off.*

◀ *The roadster featured a one-piece bench-style front seat and a unique "banjo" steering wheel adapted to fit the Volkswagen column. Note the considerable strengthening built into the door opening to make up for the removal of the roof.*

▶ *The roadster was fitted with a special dual-carburetor engine but the conversion was not tremendously successful as it suffered from "flat-spots" under acceleration. Large rear engine lid was formed from a modified front hood.*

◀ Dutchman Ben Pon (seen third from the right) took delivery of six export Beetles—three black and three dark blue-gray—on October 16, 1947. These were the first VWs ever to be officially exported to a foreign country.

▶ Major Hirst was keen to explore the possibility of selling the VW abroad and took every opportunity to promote the car at trade exhibitions. This is an export sedan, complete with chrome-plated bumpers and hubcaps.

◀ Watch out! A rather obviously staged photograph shows how the Beetle might be used by the Police, and was probably utilized as part of a road safety campaign. Poor semi-matt paint finish suggests this was a very early postwar model.

▲ Taken in a park in Hannover, this is one of a series of publicity photographs taken in 1947 which featured an export model and a number of smartly dressed young ladies. Note that even the external horn was chrome-plated.

Chapter 5

BUILDING THE BUG
So you thought the Beetle was a German car?

If you stopped anybody in the street and asked them where the Volkswagen Beetle was built, the chances are that they would reply "Germany". That would certainly be true but, there again, it would be only half the answer.

In reality, the Beetle has been built in no fewer than 20 countries around the world: Germany (at Wolfsburg, Emden, Hannover, Ingolstadt, and Osnabrück), Belgium, Portugal, Mexico, Costa Rica, Peru, Uruguay, Brazil, Venezuela, South Africa, Nigeria, Eire, Yugoslavia, Malaysia, Indonesia, Thailand, The Philippines, Singapore, Australia, and New Zealand. To be fair, the factories in some of these countries were simple assembly plants, building Beetles from CKD (Completely Knocked Down) "kits" sent from Germany, but the fact remains that the Beetle was not just a "German car". Even today, the New Beetle is assembled at the Puebla plant in Mexico.

With a need to bolster the economy by exporting German-made goods to foreign markets, Volkswagen looked into ways of not only selling the Beetle abroad, but also assembling it outside Germany. Surprisingly, one

Quality has always been a prime consideration at Volkswagen and this photograph shows an inspector closely examining the freshly-applied paintwork of a 1956 Beetle. Any blemishes would mean a return trip to the paintshop.

of the first operations to be set up on foreign soil was an assembly plant in Eire, independently funded by the Irish importer in 1950; the factory remained in use until 1977. This was closely followed, in 1951, by the opening of a plant in South Africa, and then, in 1953, by another in Brazil. Others in Mexico, Australia, and New Zealand opened within a year.

Heinz Nordhoff, Volkswagen's General Director, had been determined that every Volkswagen should be built to the same high standard, no matter which factory it had come from or what market it was to be sold into. However, it's difficult to say whether he truly achieved his ambitions in this direction, for the working conditions in some of the plants left a lot to be desired.

For example, if one examines photographs of the assembly line in Nigeria (which opened in

1975), the production lines were plainly inferior to those in Wolfsburg, with parts and tools strewn across the floor—somehow one can never imagine that to have been the case at a German plant.

What is amazing, when one sees photographs of Wolfsburg at the height of Beetle production in the 1960s, is the incredible numbers in which components—and, of course, cars—were built. This was mass-production at its most impressive—but then, the Beetle was the world's best-selling car...

However, one mustn't lose sight of the fact that Beetle production was never fully computerized, with robots picking components from parts bins and installing them as cars moved slowly down the assembly lines. No, the Beetle was—and still is—a largely hand-built car. OK, so robots never suffer from that "Monday morning" feeling, or rush to get away on a Friday night, but conversely they cannot build a car with loving care.

That's where the human touch comes into its own—and that's what helps makes the Beetle so unique.

◀ This photo, taken in 1946, shows one of the giant presses used to produce the roof section. At this time, sheet steel was in short supply, which meant that roofs were stamped from two or three pieces of steel welded together.

▲ This is the way all Beetle bodyshells began life—as vast rolls of raw sheet steel fresh from the rolling mills. Once delivered to the factory, the rolls would be transported to the press shops, ready for stamping into body panels.

◀ A solitary bodyshell moves along the production line late in 1945. Already, the factory was starting to look like a real manufacturing plant, with much of the original machinery returned to the works and restored to working condition.

▲ On March 23, 1953, Volkswagen opened a new factory in São Paulo, Brazil. This photograph shows split-window Beetles on the assembly line, even though production of the "split" had ceased in Germany on March 10, 1953.

▶ In the early days, the vast majority of the assembly process was carried out by hand, including welding the floorpan together. As far as many enthusiasts are concerned, Beetles built up to the late 1950s were the best ever in terms of quality.

▼ This 1950 photograph shows completed bodyshells being mounted on fully-assembled floorpans. To the right of the picture is a pile of steering wheels, some of which are the simple three-spoke type used on standard models.

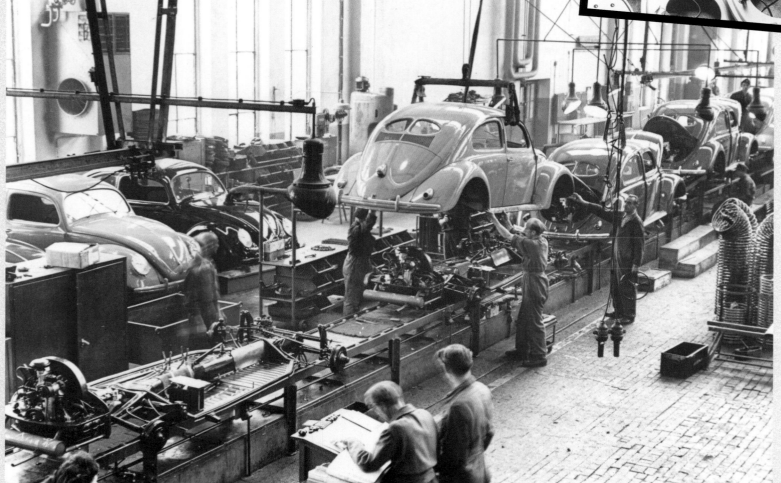

▲ Completed dashboard panels for pre-October 1952 Beetles being tested by one of the many quality-control inspectors employed by Volkswagen. Today, this batch of panels would be worth a small fortune!

◀ By the mid-1950s, finished bodyshells were generally transported around the factory by this mechanized overhead line. The photograph, taken in 1958, shows freshly painted bodies on their way to the main assembly lines.

▶ Every completed bodyshell was subjected to this test, where high-pressure jets of water were sprayed directly at the windows to check for leaks. This photograph was taken in 1947, proving that build quality was always a prime consideration.

▶ Volkswagen always offered an exchange engine program, whereby your old, worn-out motor could be returned to the factory to be exchanged for a rebuilt unit. Here used engine crankcases are being line-bored ready for re-use.

▶ The air-cooled, flat-four Volkswagen engine is without doubt the most amazingly versatile motor ever built. It has been used in everything from industrial motors to aircraft, boats, and hovercraft. Here, dozens of 1192cc engines await installation.

◀ The production lines at Volkswagen have always been staffed by both men and women in almost equal numbers. The ladies shown here are installing the rubber seal which fits between the bodyshell and the floorpan.

◀ This amazing carousel was built to speed up the body assembly process. As soon as work on one shell was completed, the equipment would rotate to bring the next into position. This was a major advance on the old "in-line" process.

◀ One inspector (right foreground) checks a freshly assembled gearbox, while another (center left) discusses a possible problem with one of the assembly workers. VW gearboxes soon earned themselves an enviable reputation for reliability.

◀ Some welding operations continued to be carried out by hand, even as late as the early 1960s. Here, a worker spot-welds part of the windshield frame assembly. This hand-finishing is part of the reason why older cars are so well built.

▲ An artistic photograph, taken in 1961, showing completed front sections of bodyshells. Separate body sections like this were brought together for final assembly using the innovative carousel shown in the previous photograph.

▶ Every Beetle from 1949 received a phosphate dip to help prevent rust. This simple process ensured every part of the bodyshell received attention, including the insides of all double-skinned sections. This is why so many old Beetles have survived.

► *Flying Beetles! Fresh from the paintshop, this collection of bodyshells awaits its turn on the main assembly lines. The photograph was taken in 1955 and it's interesting to note the irregular mix of body colors.*

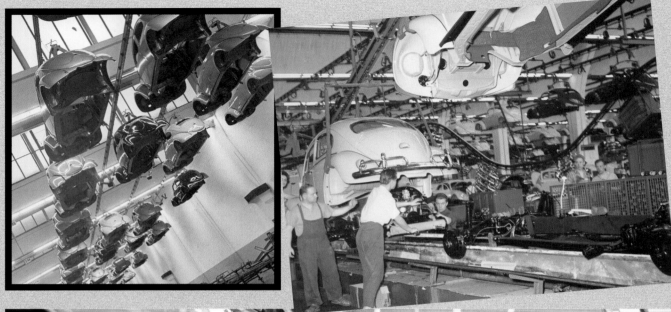

◄ *This 1960 photograph shows a bodyshell being mated to its chassis. The bodyshell next in line reveals that door trim panels and some carpets are already fitted at this stage, whereas floorpan carpets would be added later.*

► *This photo, taken in 1972, shows how little the production process changed—the cars were even built on production lines that dated way back to the 1940s. These are 1302 "Super Beetles", identifiable by their MacPherson strut front suspension.*

The fully-trimmed bodyshell of a 1303 "Super Beetle" (note the curved windshield) is bolted to its chassis. These cars were far more time-consuming to build than earlier models, largely because of their more complex front suspension.

▶ Installation of minor body parts, such as rear light assemblies, was frequently a labor-intensive operation. This 1964 Beetle is receiving attention from no fewer than four workers, and is clearly still a long way from completion.

▶ Window glass had to be installed by hand, using the time-honored trick of inserting a piece of string into the seal and pulling each end to slip the rubber into place. The Beetle shown has been fitted with American-specification bumper guards.

▲ The paint finish on this 1967 Beetle is second to none—just look at that shine! All body trim has been installed, with the exception of the side moldings. These were left until later to avoid accidental damage.

▶ Prior to leaving the factory, each car would be run up on a rolling-road (or chassis dyno) to check the engine output and braking efficiency. Headlamp alignment would also be checked using special optical equipment.

▲ Installing the interior was one of the last stages in the assembly process. Great care had to be taken not to damage any paintwork or mark the upholstery—otherwise quality control inspectors would instantly reject the car.

▶ Volkswagen had its own test facility where new models were put through their paces. This 1958 Beetle was equipped with a so-called "fifth-wheel" timing device, used to measure acceleration and top speed.

▲ During the 1970s and 1980s, crash-worthiness became a major consideration. This photograph shows the results of a side-impact test: the technician is pointing out where the hinge has been torn from the door pillar.

▲ Taken in 1973, this photograph shows just how varied was the range of vehicles produced at Wolfsburg. Included in this line-up are a few of the then-new 1303 models, a 412 Variant (or "Squareback"), a Type 3 1600 Variant, and a Type 3 "Notchback".

▶ At 11:19 A.M. on June 1, 1974, the very last Beetle to be built at Wolfsburg left the assembly line—truly the end of an era. Production continued at Emden, but already the writing was on the wall for European-built Beetles.

◀ Although January 19, 1978, marked the last day that the Beetle sedan was built in Germany, the cabriolet continued to be assembled at the Karmann factory in Osnabrück, alongside the water-cooled Golf, until January 10, 1980.

Chapter 6
THE BOOM YEARS
The humble Beetle takes on the world

The Dutch entrepreneur, Ben Pon, played a major part in the early success of Volkswagen, his order for six cars in 1947 having been the first export order ever received by the factory. Unfortunately, on the day he came to collect his vehicles, only five were actually ready, the sixth having been a victim of the erratic assembly lines.

But this wasn't Pon's only contribution to safeguarding the future of Volkswagen for, in January 1949, he sailed to the United States aboard the "Westerdam", a freighter which contained a very important cargo—the first Beetle ever to be exported to the United States.

Heinz Nordhoff realized how important it was for VW to earn income from abroad, with American Dollars always being the currency of choice. He asked Pon if he would oversee the promotion of the Beetle in the United States with a view to selling the car there. The "Westerdam" arrived on January 17 and a colleague of Ben Pon arranged a press conference on board to help publicize the Volkswagen. Unfortunately Pon met with considerable resistance; many people viewed the VW as Hitler's dream car and of little interest to the American public. Pon even tried to call the

A jubilant Nordhoff (right) celebrates the completion of the 1,000,000th Beetle on August 5, 1955. This vehicle, which is now on display at the VW Museum, was decorated with garish diamanté trim, gold paintwork, and embroidered upholstery.

car the "Victory Wagen", but it was no use— America was not yet ready for the VW.

Once ashore, the car fared no better and Pon was unable to convince the American public of its worth. The problem was, so he discovered, that the average American held most imported vehicles in poor regard. This skepticism was based on a reputation for unreliability which, in turn, was brought about largely by a poor service network and a shortage of spares. Eventually, Pon was forced to sell the car and a few spares for just $800, so that he could settle his hotel bill and pay for his return fare.

Nordhoff was disappointed and decided to travel to the United States himself to see what could be done. Much to his dismay, he met with the same mistrust of all things foreign. Then, a little over a year later, Nordhoff renewed his efforts to sell the VW into America by appointing

a sales agent, Max Hoffman, who was a successful importer of European sports cars. With responsibility for the eastern half of the United States, Hoffman eventually succeeded in selling 330 cars in 1950.

Although early sales in the United States were erratic, they inspired Nordhoff to push for greater things. Unfortunately, Hoffman's real interest lay solely in selling cars to other dealers, who would then be forced to assume responsibility for service back-up. This was at odds with Nordhoff's ideals, so, in 1953, he decided to appoint two new sales representatives: Geoffrey Lange took charge of all territories to the west of the Mississippi, and Will Van de Kamp those to the east.

Between them, Lange and Van de Kamp did a fine a job of promoting the Beetle in the lucrative American market. In April 1955, Volkswagen of America was set up, under the watchful eye of Carl Hahn, a man who shared Nordhoff's ideals. Hahn placed great emphasis on developing an efficient service and spares network, helping to create Volkswagen's legendary aftersales organization, which soon became the envy of other manufacturers throughout the world.

▲ A famous image, and rightly so, for it shows Ben Pon (left) supervising the unloading of the first Beetle ever to be officially exported to the United States, in January 1949. However, press and public opinion was against what was still perceived to be "Hitler's Car".

◀ On home territory, though, the Beetle was a huge success. It represented a sense of new-found freedom after years of deprivation under the Nazi regime and the ravages of World War II. These four ladies clearly enjoy life with their 1952 cabriolet.

◀ The Beetle blossomed from being a rather plain-Jane utilitarian vehicle into something altogether more attractive. Bill Collins' restored 1951 ragtop (sunroof) sedan is a perfect example of one of the early Export models.

▲ Despite many other refinements, the engines of early cars remained largely unchanged from the days of the wartime Schimmwagens and Kübelwagens. With a capacity of just 1131cc, they produced a modest 25 horsepower.

▶ Export or die! This postwar British slogan was also the philosophy at Volkswagen in the early 1950s. For the company to survive, it was vital to earn income from abroad. To this end, VW always put on an impressive display at motor shows, as here at Frankfurt in 1951.

◀ Heinz Nordhoff, who became General Director in January 1948, was the man largely responsible for Volkswagen's export success. It was he who insisted on establishing an efficient service network before selling automobiles in a new market—a policy first introduced by the British Board. No spares, no cars.

▲ Building the 1,000,000th Beetle was just cause for celebration for, less than ten years earlier, the future of the Volkswagen factory had looked very bleak indeed. Here, Nordhoff —just visible in front of the Beetle—makes a presentation to the world's press.

◀ The Hebmüller two-seat roadster could have been a great success for Volkswagen, but a fire at the coachbuilder's factory in July 1949 spelled the beginning of the end for this once-prestigious company. Just 696 "Hebs" were built.

◀ In notable contrast to the Hebmüller, the Karmann-built Beetle cabriolet continued in production until January 1980 and became one of Volkswagen's many success stories. The association with Karmann continues to this day, with the construction of the Golf cabriolet.

▶ Few could deny that a Beetle cabriolet is the perfect way to enjoy the California sunshine. Karmann's cabriolet became extremely popular in the United States, where its chic looks and excellent build quality soon came to be appreciated.

▲ One of the major reasons why the cabriolet proved so successful was that it remained a full four-seater (or five at a squeeze). Luggage space behind the rear seat made up for any lack of capacity in the trunk.

► Volkswagen went from strength to strength under Nordhoff's command. In 1956, the 10,000th Beetle destined for Norway left the assembly line and is seen here on its way to the railroad yard for delivery to the docks at Emden.

◄ Although the Beetle was well-equipped compared to most other small cars, a vast accessory industry grew up around it. The interior of the author's 1951 model shows many extras, including a roof storage net and parcel shelf.

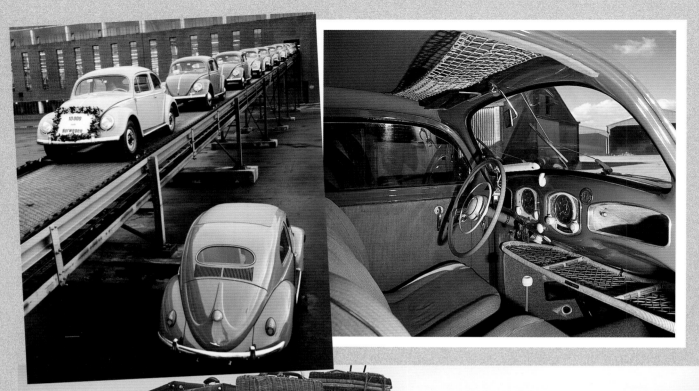

► If the Beetle suffered from anything, it was a lack of luggage space. However, that could be easily solved by the installation of a roof rack and careful selection of suitably-sized suitcases to fit in the trunk. Fender flag allows the driver to gauge the car's width when parking.

▲ Many other accessories were less useful and designed to give the impression that the Beetle was a more luxurious car. Fender skirts—usually from the American Foxcraft company—helped to give a "big car" look.

▶ In 1954, the Beetle's engine was enlarged to 1192cc and the power output increased to a mighty 36 horsepower! It may not sound much, but the new motor was one of the most reliable units VW ever produced.

▶ Everywhere there seemed to be cause for celebration. Sales in Scandinavia—Sweden in particular—exceeded all expectations. The ruggedness of the Beetle meant that the car was ideally suited to Scandinavia's harsh climate and poor road conditions.

▲ Taken in August 1960, this photograph shows a typical provincial VW dealership in Germany. The signs around the showroom extol the virtues of the new Export model, with its 40-horsepower engine and fully-synchronized transmission.

▶ The Beetle became popular in every walk of life and its form began to appear in all kinds of promotional imagery. These young ladies are showing off the new steering wheel fitted to Export models from August 1959.

▲ These two ▶ images, taken in 1958, show an Export ragtop (sunroof) sedan in rural Germany. Once again, the photographs convey a sense of freedom and hope, and a belief that bad times were a thing of the past.

▲ Volkswagen's factory at Kassel produced transmission and steering components for the Beetle. The parking lot in this 1965 photograph shows how loyal most workers were to their employers—maybe a concessionary price structure helped!

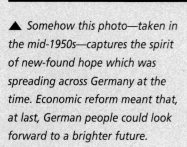

▲ Somehow this photo—taken in the mid-1950s—captures the spirit of new-found hope which was spreading across Germany at the time. Economic reform meant that, at last, German people could look forward to a brighter future.

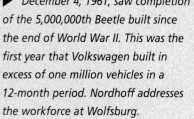

▶ December 4, 1961, saw completion of the 5,000,000th Beetle built since the end of World War II. This was the first year that Volkswagen built in excess of one million vehicles in a 12-month period. Nordhoff addresses the workforce at Wolfsburg.

▶ In 1964, Pope Paul VI blessed a line of Beetles which were ready to be exported to the United States. It's doubtful whether any car in history, other than perhaps a Ferrari, has received such Papal attention.

▲ The long and the short of it! When America's tallest man proved he could fit behind the wheel of a Beetle, Volkswagen was quick to capitalize on the publicity potential. Many new owners have been amazed at how much room there is in a Bug.

▶ Wolfsburg street scene circa 1971 and, as one might expect, there's no shortage of Volkswagens to be seen. Alongside the many Beetles are several K70s, Volkswagen's first—and ultimately ill-fated—venture into water-cooled cars.

▶ In 1962, Volkswagen of America opened new headquarters at Englewood Cliffs, New Jersey. It's surprising, though, that an assembly plant was never built in the United States.

◀ A new Beetle being hoisted aboard a freighter in 1975. Export markets continued to be profitable for Volkswagen, although sales in Germany had started to decline by this time. Three years later, all sedan production would be switched to South America.

▲ American dealerships flourished through the 1960s. This is the clinically-clean workshop of Mel Croan Motors, Inc. in Houston, Texas. The service department had no fewer than 20 work stalls, 16 of them equipped with hoists.

◀ Volkswagen exported so many vehicles that it even purchased its own ships, which sailed out of Emden. Several hundred Beetles are seen here lined up at the dockside, bound for North America.

◀ In a pause between takes, a young Sophia Loren poses with a 1961 cabriolet on a film set in France. Beetles often made brief appearances in films, particularly in the 1960s, long before Disney's "Herbie" films arrived on the scene.

◀ The parking lot of Volkswagen headquarters at Wolfsburg in July 1972 was crammed, not surprisingly, with VWs and the occasional Audi. The owner of the solitary Peugeot was a brave man to drive to work each day and park among the VWs!

▲ Even the Belgian royal family drove a Volkswagen. Such was the classless nature of the Beetle that everyone, from kings to commoners, felt at ease behind the wheel of a Bug. No other car has ever been so universally accepted.

Chapter 7

AROUND THE WORLD
The Beetle becomes everybody's favorite car

The Beetle's sales figures throughout the 1950s chart the amazing success story that has made it the car of the Millennium. No other vehicle in history—not even Henry Ford's beloved Model T—has come remotely close to matching Volkswagen's sales record.

In 1950, there were no fewer than 81,979 Beetles produced—in itself an amazing figure considering that, in 1949, a little over one half of that number of cars had been produced in the year (46,146 units). However, the production figures continued to climb at an amazing rate: 93,709 in 1951, 333,190 in 1955 and 575,407 in 1959. The first "million year" was 1965, when a total of 1,090,863 Beetles left the Volkswagen assembly lines.

With production figures continuing to rise year on year up until 1974, when they showed a marked drop (coinciding with the launch of the new water-cooled Golf model), it was inevitable that the Beetle would eventually smash all production records. On February 17, 1972, the Beetle officially stripped the Ford Model T of its title of being the world's most successful car. Altogether, an amazing 15,007,034 Beetles had

This Beetle, said to be the third postwar car built, was paraded by a German VW dealership in 1955 to celebrate the sales of over a million Beetles since World War II. Does this rare vehicle still survive?

been built, making it the world's number one! Years later, Japanese manufacturer Toyota tried to claim number one status with its Corolla model but it didn't take long for people to point out that the latest Corolla bore no resemblance to the original—unlike the Bug, whose design can clearly be traced back to the 1930s.

Despite a steady fall in production levels as worldwide demand for the Beetle took a tumble—partly as a result of VW's lack of investment in the model, which failed to keep up with customer demands for higher levels of specification, and partly due to the Beetle's inability to meet more stringent safety and emission rulings—the Beetle continued to notch up sales which saw it break through the 20,000,000 mark on May 15, 1981. With production continuing in Mexico and Brazil, rather than Wolfsburg, there was something rather special about breaking the "twenty

million" barrier and Volkswagen recognized this by offering a special silver limited edition model.

One of the Beetle's keys to success was its amazing reliability and ruggedness—and Nordhoff's insistence on an efficient aftersales service operation to ensure cars could be kept running. In developing countries, where road conditions were frequently bad, bordering on atrocious, the Beetle really came into its own. Even in remote parts of Africa, the Beetle became a common sight, but it was South America where the Beetle really established itself as the number one choice.

In 1953, work began on building a new factory at Puebla, Mexico, which finally opened in 1954. In the first year, just 500 Beetles were assembled from CKD (Completely Knocked Down) kits sent over from Germany. This CKD program was popular at the time as it was a way to start production in a foreign country without having to make a huge financial investment in press tooling and machine shops.

However, this program worked against Volkswagen to a degree, for the Mexican government became concerned that too much of the country's wealth was being lost abroad. The answer, according to the politicians, was to demand an increase in the locally-made content of each car, a figure of some 60 per cent being achieved by 1962. This would later rise to a lofty 71 per cent by the end of the 1970s.

History has now come a half-circle: once the only cars available in South America were those built in Germany, but, today, the only air-cooled Beetles available in Germany (imported and sold through independent dealers) are those built in Mexico.

But Mexico wasn't the only South American country to build the Beetle: a factory in Peru produced Beetles between 1966 and 1987, and private importers assembled them in Costa Rica (1970-75), Venezuela (1963-81), and Uruguay (1961-82). However, the most significant "rival" to Mexico was Brazil.

On March 23, 1953, Volkswagen do Brasil SA opened a new factory at São Bernado do Campo, near São Paulo, to manufacture Beetles. Between 1953 and 1957, a modest 2,268 Beetles were built at the plant, but it had become obvious that there was potential for further expansion. In 1957, permission was given to build a new VW factory, but, although it was completed the following year, no Beetles left the assembly line until January 1959. The official opening ceremony, conducted by President Kubitscheck, did not take place until November of that year.

With a domestic content of around 54 per cent, the "Fusca", as the Beetle was called in Brazil, sold well and helped satisfy the Brazilian government's desire for a more favorable import/export trade balance. On July 4, 1967, the 500,000th Fusca left the assembly line.

However, the Beetle was not the only car to be assembled in Brazil: Type 2s had been built there since 1953, and, in the 1970s, there was a whole range of unique vehicles on offer. These included the Brasilia (a popular "hatchback" model), the SP-2 sports car, a four-door Fastback, and even a special version of the Karmann Ghia coupe built at Karmann's own Brazilian factory.

In 1972, a total of 223,453 Fuscas were sold, representing approximately half of all vehicle sales for that year—this was in addition to a further 6,000 cars that had been exported. By June 1976, some 2,000,000 Brazilian Beetles had been built, with examples being exported to as many as 60 countries.

However, the boom couldn't last and, with sales flagging to 34,000 in 1984 (still an impressive figure by many manufacturers' standards!), the decision was finally taken to halt production of the Fusca. The last vehicle rolled off the line on December 7, 1986, after a total production run of 3,300,000 since the opening of the new assembly line in 1959.

However, there is an amazing twist to the story of Brazil's relationship with the Beetle, for, on February 4, 1993, the government signed a document which allowed the state-funded car industry, Autolatina, to support the re-introduction of the Fusca! The government had become concerned that there were no inexpensive cars on sale in Brazil other than cheap Japanese imports—hardly the way to help the economy. A target of 24,000 cars per year was set and soon achieved.

In hindsight, this unusual situation was not as strange as it may seem, for the condition of roads in Brazil was still terrible, with only 9 per cent of the 93,000 miles of highway being

paved. Only a car as rugged as the Beetle (or an expensive four-wheel-drive vehicle) stood a chance of surviving in such conditions.

Elsewhere in the world, the Beetle became something of an icon, revered by designers as representing the perfect embodiment of "function over form". It became the most famous car of all time, a vehicle which could be instantly recognized in any country around the globe. It was classless—a Beetle cabriolet would look equally at home outside a high-class restaurant in Paris as it would in a back street of Hong Kong—and grew to be a symbol of non-conformity, despite its success as the best-selling car of all time. After all, what better way for the child of a wealthy aristocrat to make a statement against the Establishment than to drive a car designed for the common people?

The ultimate accolade for this car of the Millennium had to be its adoption by the Walt Disney studios as the star in a series of films, commencing with "The Love Bug", starring Herbie, a white rag-top (sunroof) sedan. Herbie won a place in the hearts of millions, with his ability to do battle on the behalf of good against evil, and spawned hundreds—if not thousands—of replicas, built by devoted enthusiasts wishing to share part of the Herbie magic.

The Beetle—there will simply never be another car quite like it!

Everybody loves Herbie, the Beetle popularized by a series of Disney films. Photo copyright Walt Disney Productions

► A Beetle is loaded aboard a Dakota freight plane in South America during the 1950s. Barely a decade after the end of World War II, the Beetle was making an impact around the world, with sales figures climbing in every market.

▲ The popularity of the Beetle knew no bounds, so what could be more natural than Lufthansa—Germany's national airline—using Beetles as ground support vehicles?

► During the 1950s, it seemed that whenever a street parade was held anywhere in the world, a Beetle had to form part of the celebrations! This parade, which took place in Munich in 1953, featured a full-size cabriolet escorted by a half-size sedan.

▶ In August 1952, Volkswagen exhibited at the Canadian National Exhibition. Such was the response to the Beetle that, in September 1952, VW founded an operation to help promote sales of the Beetle in this lucrative (and snowy!) market.

▼ Taken on October 30, 1958, this photograph shows the parking lot at the VW factory in Kassel. What's interesting is that there are at least three "split window" Beetles in the line-up, with just one of the latest "big window" models.

▼ *The Beetle's ruggedness was a key to its success. Thanks to relatively high ground clearance, smooth underside, and excellent traction (afforded by the rear-mounted engine), the car was a popular choice in regions where roads left a lot to be desired.*

▶ *The British market was an important one for Volkswagen. This is the reception area at VW's import center at Ramsgate, Kent, showing three of the stylish Karmann Ghia coupes rubbing shoulders with Beetles. The two cars in the foreground bear Irish license plates.*

BOW SUMMIT
ELEV. 6,785

▲ To demonstrate just how tough the Beetle was, these three cars took part in a long-distance event in Mexico in the early 1950s, taking in all kinds of roads. The event was a success and helped to further the VW cause in this potentially huge market.

▼ In 1954, construction work began on a new factory at Puebla, Mexico, where Beetles would continue to be produced right up until the present day. At the time, few would have believed that, one day, a car called the New Beetle would be built here.

▲ In many parts of South America, dirt roads were more common than asphalt highways, especially in the 1950s and 1960s. A South American Beetle kicks up the dust while travelling at speed "south of the border".

▶ The Beetle
▼ soon became
a part of life in
Mexico, where
its popularity
grew to
almost religious
proportions.
It was to
provide
transport for
the masses in
Mexico, just
as Hitler had
wished in
prewar
Germany.

▶ Mexican street scene in 1979.
With the exception of the cabriolet,
Beetle production had ceased in
Germany in 1978, leaving the South
American factories to keep the
Beetle legend alive.

▲ A year or so earlier, this is the sight one could have expected to see at Emden as Beetles were shipped from Germany across the Atlantic, but, in 1979, the roles were reversed as South America sent cars back to Europe.

▶ From its modest beginnings, the Beetle grew to be a world-beater. On February 17, 1972, the Beetle became the best-selling car of all time, while on May 15, 1981, the 20,000,000th example rolled off the assembly line at Puebla, Mexico.

◀ A sign of changing times? A solitary Beetle bodyshell moves overhead while, down below, new Golf/Rabbit models are given their final inspection. This photograph, taken in Puebla, also shows a Type 2 (van) and several Trekkers and Brasilias.

▶ Rio's famous Copocabana is the setting for the start of this stop-light line-up. On the front row are three 1960s Beetles and a DKW, while a Citroën is on the second row. Clearly, the Brazilians liked their European cars.

◀ Unlike Henry Ford, who told his customers they could have their cars in any color as long it was black, Volkswagen offered Beetles in a wide range of hues. Check this Beetle "Harlequin", a multi-colored special model from South America!

▼ Bare bodyshells—not even in primer—are shown arriving fresh from the welding shop before being directed to the paintshop for spraying. Bodyshells were sprayed complete with doors and fenders in place.

▶ Brazilian-built Beetles are interesting in that they came with small side windows, a design feature that was superseded in August 1964 in Europe. Aside from that detail, this photograph could easily have been taken at Wolfsburg.

▶ Just out of the paintshop, this Brazilian Beetle can be seen having its wiring harness installed, a job that has to be done by hand. Although the front bumper has been fitted, all other body trim will be installed at a later stage.

◀ A colorful display of body panels fresh from the paintshop. In the background are bare Brasilia bodyshells while, in the foreground, are several dozen Beetle fenders and hoods. Red, yellow, and white are obviously popular colors in Brazil!

◀ Brazilian workers, in 1965, assembling a series of 1300cc engines ready for installation in Beetles. All Beetle engines were (and still are) put together by hand, arguably part of the reason why they are so reliable.

▶ Hundreds of Brazilian taxis line up for a special presentation. The People's Car became the most popular vehicle for use as a taxi in South America—front passenger seats are often removed to make space for luggage.

Fusca

◀ In December 1986, the Beetle (or "Fusca", as it is known in Brazil) ceased production, but only for seven years—manufacture resumed on August 23, 1993. The new cars came with 1600cc dual-carburetor motors.

◀ Although the Karmann Ghia was made in Germany, a Brazilian-built version was also on offer in South America. It differed in several details: most notable are the wheels, taillights, and bumpers.

▲ The Beetle was just one of several models produced in Brazil—the full range included these 1600 Fastback sedans and the Brasilia. All were rear-engined and air-cooled and were, technologically speaking, descendants of the Beetle.

▲ The Brasilia was a success story, offering modern styling and packaging with traditional Beetle reliability. This example has been converted to run on alcohol, a fuel which became commonplace in South America due to the high cost of regular gas.

◀ Look closely at this ghost drawing of a Brazilian-built VW Gol (yes Gol, not Golf!) and you should just be able to make out the front-mounted Beetle engine, cooled by a Porsche-style fan. Styling was reminiscent of the VW Polo.

▶ Conditions in the Nigerian VW factory in 1978 bore a close resemblance to those in Wolfsburg after World War II, with crowded assembly lines and modest tooling. Note that the engines are not equipped with heat exchangers.

▲ Despite the relatively poor working conditions; great emphasis was—and still is—placed on quality. Here, a Nigerian inspector closely examines the paintwork of a freshly-sprayed bodyshell to check for imperfections.

▶ A South African street scene in May 1979, the final year of Beetle production in that country. Volkswagen began building Beetles in South Africa back in 1951 and, to this day, continues to assemble water-cooled models.

▼ No matter where you go, or whatever the road conditions, you're bound to find a Beetle somewhere—even if it's up in the Alps in the thick of winter. Who needs four-wheel drive when you can have a Beetle with snow chains?

◀ In 1979, news that production of the Beetle cabriolet was due to end, early the following year, led to a demonstration by enthusiasts at Wolfsburg. The slogan on the banner reads "Save the Beetle Cabrio".

▶ Wherever you go in the world, you'll find enthusiasts dedicated to keeping the Beetle alive. In England, the Stanford Hall VW show has become the mecca for enthusiasts wishing to parade their vintage Volkswagens.

◀ In Germany, the Bad Camberg meeting takes place every four years, traditionally at the VW dealership of Willi Lotterman. It has grown to be the largest gathering of old Volkswagens, attracting visitors from all over the world.

▲ Fresh off the ship and ready for sale to a new owner, this Mexican-built Beetle sits on the forecourt of a German garage. Will these "modern" Beetles become collector items in years to come?

▶ An estimated 227,881 students—all fans of The Beatles pop group—signed this Beetle at the 1965 Los Angeles Fair in Hollywood, California, before it was given to a local charity. Let's hope it didn't get caught in the rain!

▶ When Diane and Alayne Emrey of Bethlehem, Pennsylvania, got married in 1965, half their guests arrived in Volkswagens—much to the couple's surprise! Surely, this must have been a marriage made in heaven?

▲ At Boston's "Maine Day" parade in 1961, a Beetle cabriolet was used to transport three local beauty queens. The cars were provided by the New England VW distributor, Hansen-MacPhee Engineering.

◀ In Denver, Colorado, a building contractor advertised his houses as having "four-car" garaging! The photo appeared in his advert in the Denver Post in 1964.

▼ The Goodyear Tire and Rubber Company used this 1965 Beetle to test its tubeless tires to the limits. The fifth "outrigger" wheel prevented the car from tipping over during this extreme test.

◄ When W. J. Mewlin of Wilmington, Delaware, went fishing, he packed his 1955 sedan with enough tackle to last a month! Included in his luggage was a 25-horsepower outboard motor—not for his Bug but for his boat...

▲ This Beetle was fully equipped with hand controls to enable John Smischny to drive, despite being paralyzed from the waist down. An ingenious system of levers allowed him to operate most functions with just one hand.

◀ Miss California of 1964 was only five years old (see inset) when the 1945 Beetle to her right was built. Competition Motors used this eye-catching photograph to draw people to its display at the Los Angeles Auto Show.

▲ When automobiles were banned from the North Sea island of Borkum, one Volkswagen owner refused to give up his favorite car. Instead, he sliced it in two and turned it into a "one horsepower" model.

▼ Montgomery, Alabama, Police Department appreciated the low running costs of a Volkswagen sedan. With the money it saved by buying a Beetle, the department then went and bought a VW truck!

▶ Lyle Ozmun Motors built this Beetle out of spare parts held in stock at their Dallas, Texas, dealership. Using parts from no fewer than eight different years of Beetle, the company put the vehicle on display in its showroom. Does it still exist?

Political rivalry led these two Beetle owners to dress up their Volkswagens to show support for their favorite candidates. The "LBJ Special" features the future President's trademark hat, while the Goldwater fans preferred to add a pair of spectacles.

▲ This pharmacy in Georgia used a Beetle to deliver drugs around the local area. Altogether, the car covered over 115,000 miles in its role as a delivery vehicle and was known locally as the "Beetle with a Big Heart".

▶ All good things have to come to an end—or do they? Ferry Porsche, son of Ferdinand, poses alongside the new VW Golf, which could so easily have been the Beetle's successor. However, the Beetle refuses to die and lives on around the world.

Chapter 8

SELLING THE VW

Step this way... Have I got a deal for you!

Of all the promotional campaigns in automotive history, there is one which stands head and shoulders above all others: the legendary series of advertisements dreamed up by the American advertising agency, Doyle Dane Bernbach. DDB's approach to advertising turned accepted principles on their heads—the adverts were self-deprecating, apparently poking fun at the product, yet, in reality, doing just the opposite. They made people sit up and take notice, not only of the advertising copy but the product itself. Who, by the end of the 1960s, hadn't been made fully aware of the Beetle's virtues?

But, memorable though DDB's advertising was—and who can possibly forget the classics such as "Lemon" or "Will we ever kill the Bug?"—it's important not to forget that the process of trying to sell the Beetle to a somewhat skeptical public began many years before DDB became involved with Volkswagen in 1959. In fact, as far back as 1947, there was a series of publicity photographs taken to show off the new "Export" model, photos which showed elegantly dressed models posing with a Beetle in a public garden in the town of Hannover.

One of the first campaigns to promote the sale of the Beetle was undertaken while VW was still under British military control. This is one of a series of photographs of an Export model taken in Hannover in 1947.

With the production lines in full swing once more, Major Ivan Hirst realized that, for the company to have a long-term future, it would be necessary to sell the Beetle into foreign markets. One of his first ventures in this respect was to visit the 1947 International Motor Show in Paris, where he and Colonel Charles Radclyffe took the opportunity not only to promote the Beetle, but also to establish a fair price for it. Ironically, of all the cars on display, the Beetle's nearest rival on price and specification appeared to be the Skoda—and Skoda now forms part of the Volkswagen organization.

The first major salon at which Volkswagen displayed its full product line was the 1951 Frankfurt Motor Show, where the company's breathtaking display was the focal point of the whole event.

However, the 1950s will be best remembered by the VW cognoscenti as being the decade of

the most beautiful promotional artwork ever seen—the brochures designed by artist Bernd Reuters. Reuters was undoubtedly the most talented of all commercial artists, a fact borne out by the way in which his artwork has become collectible even outside the VW fraternity.

Reuters' illustrations showed amazingly stylized Beetles, stretched, smoothed, rounded, to the point where they resembled coachbuilt sports cars of the 1930s—yet they were still recognizably VWs. They turned the humble workers' car into something altogether more elegant and desirable. They promoted a dream.

By comparison, the brochures of the 1960s were more factual and far less impressive in their design, although they are still highly prized among collectors. It was only when the 1970s arrived that Volkswagen appeared to lose its way, with rather clinical publications that told the whole story, but not in a romantic manner.

Today, there's huge interest among VW enthusiasts who wish to collect every form of VW promotional memorabilia, but be warned: much of the material is now worth as much as a Beetle cost when new!

▶ In an effort to increase awareness of the product, Volkswagens were frequently exhibited at trade exhibitions in the late 1940s. Here the intricacies of a cut-away engine and transmission are being explained to an interested group.

▲ One of the first major auto shows at which Volkswagen had a significant presence was the 1951 Frankfurt Motor Show. This is a scale model of a proposed idea for the Volkswagen stand—the final design differed in several details.

▼ The VW display at Frankfurt in 1951 attracted a vast amount of public interest. Several cars and Transporters were displayed, many mounted at an angle to give the public an overall view of the latest Wolfsburg products.

▼ Early VW promotional literature is highly collectible—even among those who aren't VW enthusiasts. The quality of the artwork, the product of the immensely talented Bernd Reuters, sets it apart from that of contemporary rivals.

Das CABRIOLET

▲ Reuters' artwork was simply stunning in its execution. He had the ability to make even the most prosaic of vehicles look a million dollars—not that the VW could ever be accused of being prosaic! The style, the colors—everything was perfect.

◀ Reuters' ability to draw ghosted illustrations was second to none. So many of his rivals produced lifeless, almost clinical, artwork that had more the feel of an engineering drawing—Reuters created a lifestyle.

▶ *Several Volkswagens took part in this parade in Wolfsburg in 1953. Every opportunity was taken to promote the People's Car to the public—there were still relatively few privately-owned cars on the road.*

▼ *"Do you like the European look in automobiles? Are you keen on riding in easy comfort, yet would like to have a means of transport that's downright cheap to operate?" asks this U.S.-market brochure. The answer has to be "Yes!".*

SEDAN
STANDARD AND DE LUXE MODELS

field, is exactly what you are looking for. Technicians the world over say that the Volkswagen is the most sensible automobile ever built and that it is years ahead in design. The Volkswagen was designed by a genius as unique in his field as Caruso was as a tenor. The Volkswagen Sedan is built in two models, Standard and De Luxe. Both models are handsome in their shining metallic finish. The De Luxe Sedan offers a choice of bewitching colors. Expensive upholstery and handsome practical fittings blend into a harmonious whole with typical European discretion. All Volkswagen models offer the same basic features that make Volkswagens so outstanding. All have that surprisingly fast getaway, that smooth and safe driving thanks to marvelous suspension and a low center of gravity, and that extraordinary economy of operation combined with great driving comfort which characterize the Volkswagen and make it unequalled in its field.

Do you like the European look in automobiles? Are you fond of clean-cut stream-lined cars? Are you keen on riding in easy comfort, yet would like to have a means of transportation that is downright cheap to operate? If such is the case, the Volkswagen, the leading European car in its

◀ *Another example of Reuters' artwork, this time showing an early 1960s ragtop (sunroof) Beetle.*

▶ Volkswagen dealerships in Germany during the 1950s and early 1960s were somber places by comparison with the showrooms of today. Muted lighting, very little decoration, and not a billboard in sight.

◀ Dealerships were required to display a selection of models within the limitations of the space available. This dealer, in Ebingen, Germany, chose a cabriolet and a ragtop (sunroof) sedan. Tiny signs by the cars state that they are already sold.

▲ A spectacular display of fenders, each painted a different color, dominates this dealer's window. The intention was to promote Volkswagen's new range of colors for 1962. Note the Type 3 "Notchback".

▶ The new 1200A model, introduced in August 1965 alongside the new 1300 Beetles, clearly attracted great interest at this dealership. The 1300 was the flagship model while the 1200A was the "budget" Beetle.

▶ Before Volkswagen of America was formed, Max Hoffman, whose head office was in New York, was the official importer of the Beetle into the United States. This was the first sales brochure for the U.S. market.

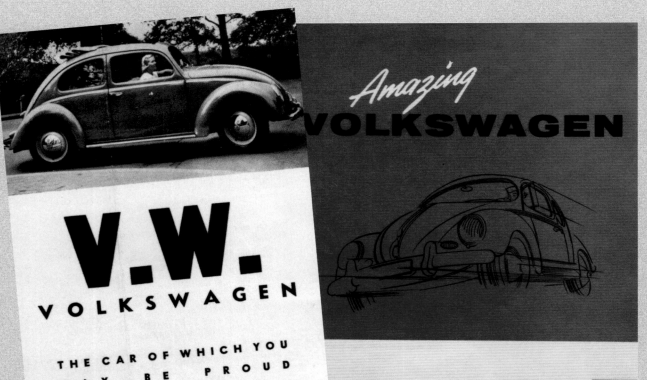

◀ In the mid-1950s, ▼ Volkswagen divided U.S. sales operations into two. The western half was headed by Geoffrey Lange, who issued a brochure (left) extolling the virtues of "America's most popular imported car". The eastern half came under the control of Will Van de Kamp, whose version (below) featured Reuters' artwork "borrowed" from the European catalogs and supported by suitable sales patter.

▶ Volkswagen's advertising of the 1960s played heavily on the improvements made to the Beetle. The VW management had often been criticized for relying too heavily on the Bug—this brochure helped to show how much it had changed.

▲ Volkswagen of America had clear ideas about what the perfect dealership should look like, and produced models to show how this could be achieved. This one is a dealership designed to sell 220 new cars a year.

▼ The completed dealership was very little different from the model. This Southern California facility was described as being "typical of medium-sized dealerships". It had approximately 8,200 square feet of floor space.

▶ By way of contrast, this dealer is "south of the border", in Mexico. The photograph, taken in 1967, shows how the corporate Volkswagen identity was applied around the world. The design of the building may have differed, but the overall image didn't.

Where are they now?

Return with us now to those wondrous days of yesteryear.

It's 1949 and automobiles are getting longer, lower and wilder.

Massive bumpers are a big hit. Fins are in. And everyone's promising to "keep in style with the times."

But then, times changed. Massive bumpers and fins went out. So did every car shown above, except the VW.

You see, back in '49, when all those other guys were worrying about how to improve the way their cars looked, we were worrying about how to improve the way ours worked.

And you know what? 2,200 improvements...

▲ *This advert asked where all the other "cars of the future", advertised in 1949, had disappeared to? Of the six cars shown—Tucker, Packard, De Soto, Studebaker, Hudson, and Volkswagen—only one survived.*

Will we ever kill the bug?

Never.

How could we? We brought the Volkswagen into the world, and gave it the best years of our life. When people laughed at its looks, we helped it make friends all over the world. 8 million of them.

And we promised them that this was one car that would never go out of style (much less out of sight).

We won't deny that the bug's been changed. But not so you'd notice. The 5,000-odd changes we've made since 1948 don't do a thing to the VW ex-cept make it work better and longer.

A few purists feel we kill the bug each time we improve it. But we have no choice. We've got to keep killing the bug every chance we get. That's the only sure way to keep it from dying.

...at's how many times we inspect a Volkswagen.

...ok's our little car ...'s from the no's. ...a look for things ...asked us what

we were going to do about a roof that came through with a dent in it.

Dents are easy to hammer out. So what we did shook him a little. We smashed the body down to a metal lump and threw it out in the scrap pile.

We stop VWs for little things that you may never notice yourself.

The fit of the lining in the roof. The finish in a doorjamb. In the final inspection alone, our VW has to get through 342 points without one blackball.

One out of 50 doesn't make it. But you should see the ones that get away.

◄ *The greatest automobile promotional campaign of all time was dreamt up in the 1960s and 1970s by the advertising agency Doyle Dane Bernbach (DDB). DDB turned advertising on its head by using headlines which appeared to poke fun at the product.*

▲ *VW was proud of its quality control operation and made frequent references to it in advertising over the years. This DDB advert told how there were 342 quality checks made on each car and that 1 in 50 VWs didn't make the grade.*

33 years later, he got the bug.

We're glad that most people don't wait 33 years to buy their first Volkswagen.

But Albert Gillis did, and maybe he had the right idea all along.

He didn't buy a new car for 33 years because he didn't happen to need one.

He and his 1929 Model A Ford did just fine by each other.

▲ In 1929, Albert Gillis bought his Model A Ford. He kept it for 33 years, until he finally gave into temptation and bought a new car—a Volkswagen of course! DDB loved the story and turned it into a press campaign.

▶ This advert suggested that it didn't matter what year Beetle you drove, they were all equal when it came to the quality and availability of replacement parts. Owners of split-window models may not quite agree with that statement today!

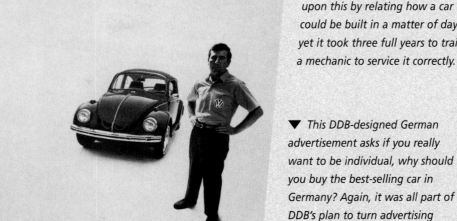

It takes a week to make the car. And 3 years to make the mechanic.

Oh the difference between a bug and a man.

In just seven days a piece of steel evolves into a sturdy Volkswagen.

But only after three years does a raw recruit evolve into a bona fide Volkswagen mechanic.

It's not an easy process.

He starts with a lowly doorknob and works his way up to the electrical system. (With an eagle-eyed supervisor over his shoulder.)

He takes every part apart. And puts it back together again. Over and over and over.

Then we clock him.

If he does the right job in the right time, bully for him.

He does it again.

Only after he passes the test twice do we feel he's mastered that part. And can go on to another.

But this is only part of the grind.

When this man's not working on the VW, we're working on him. At a Volkswagen training school.

There he spends seven hours a day in class studying about the car.

So by the end of his apprenticeship, he knows every nook and cranny in a VW.

For once, man counts as much as the machine.

◀ One of VW's strengths had always been its worldwide service network. DDB capitalized upon this by relating how a car could be built in a matter of days, yet it took three full years to train a mechanic to service it correctly.

▼ This DDB-designed German advertisement asks if you really want to be individual, why should you buy the best-selling car in Germany? Again, it was all part of DDB's plan to turn advertising theory upside-down.

Ganz gleich welchen Jahrgang Sie fahren…

wenn Ihr treuer Volkswagen nach jahrelanger Laufzeit – am Berg und beim Überholen – müde wird: Ein VW-Austauschmotor gibt ihm wieder neue Kraft.

Der VW-Austauschmotor ist praktisch ein „neuer" Motor, der im Volkswagenwerk von erfahrenen Fachleuten fabrikatorisch aufbereitet wurde. Alle zurückgegebenen gebrauchten Motoren zerlegt man dort in sämtliche Einzelteile. Unbrauchbare Teile werden unnachsichtig verschrottet. An ihre Stelle treten fabrikneue Original-VW-Ersatzteile. Am Fließband werden nun aus diesen Einzelteilen neue Motoren zusammengebaut – die VW-Austauschmotoren.

VW-Austausch-Motoren sind einbaufertig! Kraftstoffpumpe, Vergaser, Luftfilter, Lichtmaschine, Zündverteiler, Zündspule, Zündkerzen, automatische Kühlluftregelung, Auspuffanlage und Kupplung – also alle Aggregate, die zum Motor gehören – sind aufbereitet und im Preis inbegriffen.

Übrigens: Das VW-Austauschprogramm umfaßt Motoren, Getriebe und Hinterachsen, Vorderachsen, Zylinder, Zylinderköpfe, Stoßdämpfer, Geschwindigkeitsmesser – insgesamt rund 270 Teile!

VOLKSWAGENWERK AG WOLFSBURG

Sind Sie Individualist genug, den meistgekauften Wagen Deutschlands zu kaufen?

Finden Sie es albern, ein gutes Auto nur deswegen nicht zu kaufen, weil Millionen Leute es auch gut finden?

Haben Sie es nicht auch lieber, wenn man sich nach Ihnen statt nach Ihrem Auto umdreht?

Ist es Ihnen egal, daß jeder weiß, wie wenig ein VW kostet?

Sind Sie der Meinung, daß ein Auto für Sie arbeiten sollte und nicht umgekehrt?

Stecken Sie Ihr Geld lieber in Hobbies anstatt in Autos, die Ihnen kein Geld mehr für Hobbies lassen?

Dann sind Sie Individualist genug, um sich den Käfer kaufen zu können.

Wir wahren die Form. Bis zum Schluß.

Über die Form des Käfers gab es keine Diskussion. Sie war vernünftig. Sie war praktisch. Sie war verblüffend einfach. Und sie verkörperte eine einmalige Idee.

Natürlich haben wir am Käfer im Laufe der Zeit fast alle Äußerlichkeiten korrigiert. Weil wir das Auto immer weiter verbessern wollten, weil's der Zeitgeschmack so mit sich brachte.

Die Grundform jedoch haben wir bis heute erhalten. Alles blieb glatt und rund an diesem Wagen. Fast 21 Millionen Käfer-Käufer auf der ganzen Welt fanden das auch völlig in Ordnung.

Jetzt verabschiedet sich die erfolgreichste Automobilform aller Zeiten. In Gestalt von 2.400 exklusiv ausgestatteten Käfern.

Und in der Erfolgsspur des Käfers längst ein anderer Volkswagen: der Inzwischen schon über 7 millionenmal kauft. Das meistgekaufte Auto der N Formvollendet und allseits beliebt. Ein Form von Volkswagen.

Da weiß man, was ma

▲ One of the classic DDB advertisements in Europe compared the shape of the Beetle with an egg—one of the most perfect forms in nature.

▶ Another advert emphasizing the money-saving nature of a Beetle. Only in Germany, it says, do 2,099 millionaires save money with this car. The Volkswagen— truly a classless car, driven by millionaires and paupers alike!

Der VW 1200. Wie können wir ihn so billig machen, ohne ihn billig zu machen?

Der VW 1200 kostet unverändert 4484,70 Mark ab Werk. Einschließlich 407,70 Mark Umsatzsteuer.

Er ist also ein billiges Auto.

Wichtiger aber ist, daß er deswegen kein billiges Auto ist. Schauen Sie ihn sich einmal an. Sie werden sofort sehen, daß er nicht zu jenen Wagen gehört, bei denen mit Gewalt an allen Ecken und Kanten gespart wird, damit ein optisch günstiger Preis herauskommt.

Die Sitzbezüge sind zum Beispiel aus luftdurchlässigem Kunstleder. Das Dach und die Seiten haben eine Verkleidung aus abwaschbarem Kunststoff. Der Fußraum vorn ist mit einem N...

Sie finden Schraubanschlüsse für jede Art Sicherheitsgurt, drei Entfrosterdüsen an der Frontscheibe, eine pneumatische Scheibenwaschanlage, Sicherheits-Tür-verriegelungen und eine zusätzliche Heizung im Fond.

Außen hat er Zierleisten, verchromte Radkappen und breite, verchromte Stoßstangen.

Und das alles ist so solide verarbeitet, daß man dem Wagen auch nach Jahren seine Jahre nicht ansieht.

Wie können wir nun ein so aufwendiges Auto so billig verkaufen?

Je besser ein Auto ist, desto besser läßt es sich verkaufen. Und je besser sich ein Auto verkaufen läßt, desto billiger läßt es sich bauen.

Allein in Deutschland sparen 2099 Millionäre Geld mit diesem Wagen.

„Geld", so sagte mal ein bekannter Mann, „ist zu wertvoll, als daß man es unnütz ausgeben sollte." Und mit dieser Einstellung sparte er sich ein Riesenvermögen zusammen.

Tatsächlich scheint zum Reichtum eine gesunde Portion Sparsamkeit zu gehören. Wie sonst ist sonst zu erklären, daß allein in Deutschland 2099 Millionäre einen VW fahren. Dieser

Wagen hat genau das, was auch einem Millionär gefällt.

Er ist nicht teuer in der Anschaffung und im Unterhalt, kann schnell und preiswert repariert werden, muß aber selten repariert werden, läuft viele Jahre lang zuverlässig und läßt sich dann teuer wieder verkaufen.

Daß dieses Auto zwar hübsch und komfortabel, aber nicht unauffällig ist, erscheint reichen Leuten nicht als Nachteil. Wer Geld hat, braucht es nicht ständig zu zeigen.

Nun soll hier nicht der Eindruck erweckt werden, der Käfer sei nur was für Millionäre. Wir verkaufen ihn selbstverständlich auch an Leute, die es erst werden wollen.

▲ "How can we build the Beetle so cheap without making it a cheap car?"—that's the rough translation of this German advert, which set out to emphasize the amazing value for money that the Beetle represented.

◀ *Probably the best-known Volkswagen advert of all time—the "lemon" refers to this car having been rejected by the quality control team. The ad is typical of the self-denigrating material produced for Volkswagen by Doyle Dane Bernbach.*

▼ *Somehow, the later promotional material never quite matched up to the classic productions of the 1950s and 1960s. This is a brochure for the Mexican-built Beetle—it's factual but lacks the style of earlier publications.*

Lemon.

This Volkswagen missed the boat.

The chrome strip on the glove compartment is blemished and must be replaced. Chances are you wouldn't have noticed it; Inspector Kurt Kroner did.

There are 3,389 men at our Wolfsburg factory with only one job: to inspect Volkswagens at each stage of production. (3000 Volkswagens are produced daily; there are more inspectors than cars.)

Every shock absorber is tested (spot checking won't do), every windshield is scanned. Volkswagens have been rejected for surface scratches barely visible to the eye.

Final inspection is really something! VW inspectors run each car off the line onto the Funktionsprüfstand (car test stand), tote up 189 check points, gun ahead to the automatic brake stand, and say "no" to one VW out of fifty. This preoccupation with detail means the VW lasts longer and requires less maintenance, by and large, than other cars. (It also means a used VW depreciates less than any other car.)

Volkswagen plucks the lemons; you get the plums.

El Volkswagen. Reflejo de la perfección.

En muchos países, más de 20 millones de propietarios del Volkswagen, han comprobado la nobleza y perfección de este automóvil que asegura un máximo rendimiento con efectividad y así con sea la temperatura ambiente, nunca se sobrecalienta. El Volkswagen tiene suspensión independiente en las 4 ruedas, mediante barras de torsión y por lo tanto, también amortiguación independiente. Estamos...

Su resistente motor de larga vida, es de reducido consumo de combustible, tiene potencia de sobra para responder con efectividad y así cual sea la...

El Volkswagen es su conjunto, una perfecta economía, funcionalidad, comodidad, versatilidad, seguridad y alto valor de reventa. Es un automóvil...

VW El Volkswagen. *La mejor compra.*

▶ *This Brazilian "Fusca" (Beetle) brochure is a little more aesthetically pleasing in its simplicity but still lacks the "Reuters' touch". Even so, such material is still considered collectible by enthusiasts across the world.*

Fusca.
As boas idéias são simples.

◀ *Probably the finest promotional catalogs ever produced by the aftermarket were those from EMPI, of Riverside, California. Today, EMPI material is among the most highly-valued of all Volkswagen memorabilia.*

Chapter 9

THE SPECIAL ONES

Not all Beetles look the same

Even as far back as the prewar years, when the first KdF-Wagen prototypes were still undergoing final testing, Dr Ferdinand Porsche was hard at work designing special versions of his People's Car. Designs included such vehicles as light delivery vans and pickups, all based on the regular sedan.

After the war, when the factory was under the control of the British Military Government, several variations on the Beetle theme were built, ranging from box vans to ambulances. Some were produced in VW's experimental workshops, while others were the product of private concerns anxious to find work in lean times. Among them was Christian Miesen, who built a simple ambulance based on the Beetle. This had the patient on a stretcher alongside the driver.

But Miesen wasn't the only one to realize the potential of the Beetle for use by what we today know as the emergency services. Papler, Austro-Daimler, and Hebmüller each built simple, open-topped "convertibles" for use as Police vehicles, surviving examples of which are few and far between today.

Hebmüller was also responsible for building

To celebrate the assembly of the 20,000,000th Beetle, in 1981, Volkswagen launched a limited-edition model called the "Silver Bug". The 20,000,000th Beetle is shown here with the VW Museum's 1938 prototype.

what was, without doubt, one of the most attractive special-bodied Beetles ever produced: the Type 14A roadster. Sadly, production of this elegant vehicle ceased in 1953 after just 696 examples had been built. The main reason for the premature demise of the Type 14A was a fire which broke out in the Hebmüller factory one Saturday afternoon in 1949—a disaster from which the company never really recovered. The last 15 cars were actually assembled by Karmann after Hebmüller had filed for bankruptcy in 1952.

There were many other coachbuilders in the 1950s who regarded the Beetle as a perfect base on which to create a stylish sports car. Among them were Rometsch, Beutler, and Wendler, all long-established companies which, along with newcomers such as Dannenhauer & Stauss, built several interesting vehicles for wealthy clientele.

What made the Beetle so attractive for such purposes was the fact that it had a largely self-

contained chassis and driveline—it was also inexpensive and readily available, although the factory was, at times, reluctant to sell bare chassis directly to outside coachbuilders.

Without doubt the most successful, and arguably the most attractive, of all VW-based special-bodied vehicles was the Karmann Ghia, in both coupe and cabriolet styles. Launched in 1955, the Ghia, as it's colloquially known, was a hit from the very beginning. Its blend of Italian style (by Ghia of Turin, under the leadership of Luigi Segre) and German engineering (it was almost pure Beetle under the skin, with the exception of a widened floorpan) appealed to a wide audience, especially in the United States, where the Ghia was a huge success.

But the Karmann Ghia was not the only special model to be sold by the VW factory. Over the years, there have been many limited-edition Beetles built at Wolfsburg, including the denim-trimmed "Jeans Beetle", the bright yellow "Sun Bug", and the attractive "Champagne edition" cabriolet. However, underneath the skin, they were all regular Beetles. Some things you just wouldn't want to change…

▶ The Hebmüller roadster was, without doubt, one of the prettiest special-bodied Beetles ever designed. Built at Wulfrath by Joseph Hebmüller, the model received official blessing and was given the VW designation Type 14A.

▲ Hebmüllers were built by converting stock sedan bodyshells—they were sliced off along the waistline and new windshield frames and rear bodywork were then grafted into place. Considerable strengthening was also added.

VOLKSWAGEN
Cabriolet
2 Sitzer

▲ As was the case with the four-seat Karmann cabriolet, the Hebmüller's top was an extremely well-constructed affair. There was also modest accommodation for luggage or an occasional passenger.

▲ The level of interior trim on most Hebmüllers was higher than that found on stock Beetles, with leather being a popular option. Note the unusual door trim panels, complete with individual storage pockets.

▲ It's sad that the Hebmüller did not remain in production, for it was undeniably elegant. Marketed as a two-seat cabriolet, it would have made the perfect partner to the Karmann-built four-seat model.

▲ Police! Stop! The passenger of a Hebmüller Type 18A police cabriolet flags down the driver of a split-window Beetle. The Type 18A was crude, with canvas doors and bulky top. Chains across the door openings kept passengers in place.

▶ Apart from Hebmüller's Type 18A (seen here), police vehicles were also built by Austro-Daimler and Papler. The latter were also known as Type 18As but enjoyed the advantage of having steel rather than canvas doors.

◀ This Dutch-converted police vehicle was based on a 1960 Karmann cabriolet. Of special interest are the small windows let into the roof and the tonneau cover over the rear seat area. Note also the blue emergency light on the roof.

▲ An intriguing photograph, for it shows a line of 1967 European-specification Beetles equipped with U.S.-market bumpers and roof-mounted emergency lights. The paint finish is clearly matt rather than glossy. Were they destined for U.S. Forces in Germany?

A once-common sight on the roads of Germany, a police Beetle resplendent in the usual two-tone green-and-white paint finish. Beetles remained the number one choice with the German police for many years.

As many as 500 of these Krankenwagen, or ambulances, were built by Miesen until the 1960s, this example being based on a pre-May 1949 sedan. The conversion was simple, but ingenious, with folding stretchers stored in the roof box.

▲ A stretcher could be carried inside the vehicle on a table which pivoted round and slid out through the passenger door. To allow room for this, the driver's seat backrest had to be tilted forward and the door opened wider than normal.

► A prototype Beetle-based van built for the Deutsche Bundespost (German Post Office). The design is interesting as it shares certain features with the Karmann cabriolet, including a windshield with a squared-off upper edge and aluminum-framed door windows. The rear fenders appear to be modified sedan panels but the remainder of the bodywork was scratch-built, including the rear hatch and engine lid. Access to the generous loading space was hindered by the height of the engine bay. The interior was spartan, with just a seat for the driver. Note the plain "passenger side" door panel and the black three-spoke steering wheel, as fitted to Standard model Beetles.

◄ A fleet of Beetles awaits delivery to the Togo Republic's postal service in 1962. The Beetles are all Standard models (note the lack of body trim and the painted bumpers) but have been fitted with accessory pop-out rear side windows.

▶ In 1964, the Deutsche Bundespost took delivery of its 25,000th Volkswagen—the German postal service used Type 2s, as well as Beetles, for delivery work. Note the painted hubcaps, mirrors, and bumpers.

▼ Not all postal Beetles were painted yellow—some were finished in this unflattering shade of gray-green. This photograph was taken late in 1967 and shows one of the 1968 Standard models.

▶ ADAC, the German Automobile Club, relied on Beetles to provide much of its "strassenwacht" (road patrols); these aided stranded motorists or helped out in emergencies. The photo was taken in 1981 and shows a new VW Passat with the ADAC Beetle.

▲ The Deutsche Bundespost also used Trekker (Type 181) vehicles to provide service support out in the field. These robust machines were ideal for such work, being virtually indestructible. Of course, a Beetle engine helped reliability!

▶ The Karmann Ghia is undoubtedly the best known and most glamorous of the Beetle's "relatives". Its curvaceous body was styled by Luigi Segre of Ghia, seen here posing proudly alongside one of the first production models.

▶ This photograph was taken on July 14, 1955, on the occasion of the official press presentation of the new Karmann Ghia coupe. Secrecy had been so great until that point that none of the guests had any idea what they had been invited to see.

▲ From its launch to the day production finally ceased, in 1974, the Karmann Ghia was universally praised for its elegant styling. Some 362,000 coupes were built during the model's 19-year lifespan.

▼ The Karmann Ghia was built on a widened Beetle chassis after it was realized that the stock floorpan was too weak to support the wider coupe body. Also added was a front anti-sway bar, something that was not used on Beetles until the 1960 model year.

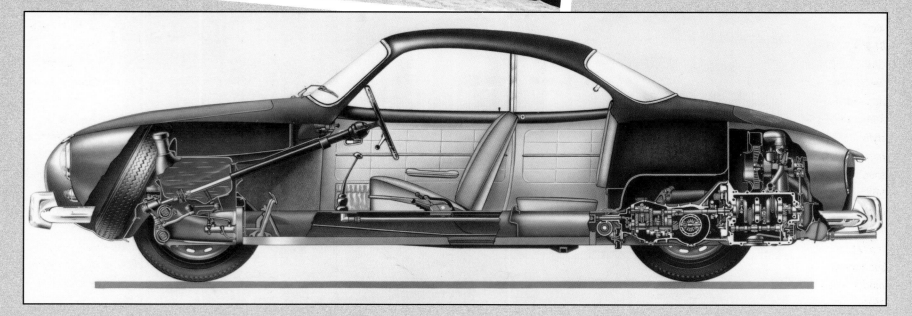

▲ Some 81,000 Karmann Ghia cabriolets were built between 1957 and 1974. This stylish roadster has become sought-after by Volkswagen enthusiasts. This example is a U.S.-specification model built in 1970.

◄ Volkswagen tried to upgrade the Karmann Ghia by introducing the Type 34, nicknamed the "Grosser (Big) Karmann Ghia" in Germany. Aimed squarely at the U.S. market, its styling was not to everyone's taste.

▶ *San Remo, Italy, September 1954—an elegant Rometsch roadster goes on parade at a Concours d'Elegance. The Rometsch, styled by Johannes Beeskow, was built by one of the best-known coachbuilders of the era.*

▼ *The Rometsch was based entirely on the Volkswagen driveline but had a number of unusual features, such as this side-facing rear seat. Note the considerable strengthening across the door opening on this early example.*

▶ *Rometsch built a second Volkswagen-based design in 1957, this time designed by Bert Lawrence. Its styling was, in many ways, reminiscent of the Chevrolet Corvette. Although a little "modern" for some tastes, the design won several awards.*

▲ *Rometsch built cars in the traditional manner, forming individual panels over a hand-crafted wooden "buck". No two bodyshells were ever precisely the same, but the quality of workmanship on each was second to none.*

◀ Several designs were considered by Rometsch, including this elegant roadster. The dashboard is very similar to that of the contemporary Karmann Ghia. Sadly, this styling exercise never made it into production.

▲ A new Rometsch nears completion. The body panels have been lifted off the wooden buck and transferred to the steel framework built on the chassis. If you look closely, it's possible to see the marks from the coachbuilders' hammers.

▲ Not all Rometschs were exotic roadsters or coupes—the company had built its reputation on constructing taxis. In 1951, the company launched a four-door Volkswagen taxi, which was some 7 inches longer than the stock Beetle.

◀ The Swiss coachbuilding concern, Beutler, built a series of very attractive coupes based on both Volkswagen and Porsche drivelines. Ultimately, the excessively high cost of production brought the series to an end around 1959.

▶ Volkswagen itself built numerous "special" Beetles, mostly to boost flagging sales figures. One of the most popular in Europe was the Jeans Beetle, which came complete with denim upholstery and blacked-out body trim.

▲ Not all special-bodied Volkswagens were beautiful. The stylist responsible for this unique coupe clearly fought against tradition when he penned this design. It was just one of a great many "one-offs" built in the 1950s.

▶ Even today, special-bodied early VWs turn up in the most unlikely of places. This example was discovered in Scandinavia and consisted of an aluminum body on the chassis of a 1943 Kübelwagen. Let's hope it will be saved one day!

▲ Not all
◀ Beetle-based specials were cars! This assault craft had a much-modified Beetle engine connected directly to the propeller via a long drive shaft.

◀ And, finally, perhaps the ultimate "special-bodied"—or rather "un-bodied"—Beetle! Built at the factory as an educational aid, this Super Beetle has been extensively cut away to demonstrate how a Beetle works.

Chapter 10
CUSTOM BUGS
Giving the Beetle that personal touch

It's probably true to say that no other car in history has been treated to "that personal touch" to the same extent as the VW Beetle. There is something about the Beetle which appears to bring out the urge in people to make their car stand out in the crowd, be it by simply adding some hand-painted flowers or by trying to turn it into some wild-looking sports car.

The craze for customizing—the art of personalizing a car—really started in the United States in the 1950s but soon spread to Europe. To begin with, it mostly took the form of installing a few of the many accessories which were available, such as dashboard-mounted bud vases to hold flowers, maybe a pair of fender skirts (for the "big car look"), some extra lighting, or simply a set of chrome wheel trims. They were all installed for the same reason: to make the Beetle stand out from the rest.

In the 1960s, the customizing scene expanded in many directions: some people endeavored to make their Beetles go as fast as they could, while others preferred to paint them in bright colors, perhaps adding some stripes or flowers for that "Woodstock Look". Then there

Hand-applied psychedelic paintwork turns a Beetle into a statement. The owner of this hippy-style Bug prefers to stand out from the crowd—not for him (or her) the ritual of washing and waxing every weekend!

were those who wished to transform their Bugs into something quite different: a stylish sports car, a tough off-road machine, or—perhaps the ultimate conversion, considering the Beetle's humble beginnings—a stretched limousine!

Of the latter, there have been several fine—and many not-so-fine—conversions carried out on both sides of the Atlantic Ocean. The best examples have been given the full works, with plush leather interiors, polished wood drinks cabinets, and dark "privacy glass". They attract attention, raise a few smiles, and, above all, thumb their noses at convention.

With regard to performance, in 1960s Southern California a whole industry grew up, intent on transforming the People's Car into a mini-Porsche. Companies like EMPI from Riverside, California, sold a huge variety of aftermarket parts for Volkswagens, ranging from high-performance engine equipment to chromed

dress-up items, which added some glitter to the plain-Jane Beetle. Wheels became a popular accessory, with dozens of companies offering aluminum or magnesium rims, which, for the most part, were sold on looks rather than practicality. And, above all, that's what customizing is all about: visual appeal. After all, few cars are more practical than a stock Beetle.

The Beetle's familiar body has been used to cloth all manner of alternative mechanical underpinnings: over the years many powerful Beetles have been built with V-8 motors, their Detroit powerplants transforming the lethargic People's Car into a power-crazed "People's Musclecar". Once again, like the limousine VW, it's a way of poking fun at conventional ways of thinking: all Beetles are slow—aren't they?

But, surely, if you wish to stand out from the crowd, you don't jump behind the wheel of the world's most popular car? But, ask any customizer and he'll tell you that there's something intensely satisfying about taking a humble car like the Bug, and turning it into something outrageous. It's called being an individual.

◄ *Which way shall we go? Built by a German dealer from two old Beetles, this "push-me-pull-you" Bug doesn't know whether it's coming or going! Thankfully, only one steering wheel is connected—but which?*

▼ *There is something wonderfully perverse about creating a limousine out of a Bug. After all, the Volkswagen was originally conceived as a car for the worker. This stretched mid-1970s example is in Holland.*

▲ *"Stretchin' Your Imagination". And that's just what this over-long cabriolet does! It's actually a cut-down and stretched sedan (the shape of the windshield is the giveaway). Wonder how it handles?*

▶ *Another variation on the limo theme, this time a more simple conversion as the doors used in the rear are unchanged from stock. The vinyl-covered roof is an easy way to cover up all the extra welding required to stretch a Beetle.*

▶ Polished Porsche wheels, rich metallic paintwork, and some tasteful pinstriping really give this "Limo-Bug" a touch of class. Judging from the photo alongside it, this one-off Beetle is pretty popular with the girls.

▲ Whoever said the interior of a Beetle is too plain? The rear of this stretched Beetle features leather upholstery, polished wood drinks cabinet, and that all-important telephone. Rear-facing seats make it a six-seater (at least!).

▶ Need more space but don't want to cut up your Bug? Then this accessory roof-rack tent is just what the doctor ordered! Made in Italy, it offers accommodation (of sorts!) for two—just don't forget to take it down before using a carwash.

▲ Now, this is the ultimate stretched Beetle. Built by the Harmening coachbuilding concern in Bückeburg, Germany, this 48-seat combination was used between 1958 and 1976 to carry sightseers around the Volkswagen factory.

118

▶ In 1964, Axel Schlesinger and A. Kuehn decided to cross the Straits of Messina—by Volkswagen! Equipped with a propeller, the Beetle made the crossing—between Italy and Sicily—at an average speed of just 4.3 miles per hour. A few years later, they did it all over again.

◀ Now, if you want to go to sea in real style, how about the Waterbug? Built by Stewart Dahlberg, of Creative Car Craft in Florida, its fiberglass Beetle bodyshell rests on a conventional hull, making it truly seaworthy.

▲ Power comes from a 50-horsepower Mariner outboard motor mounted in the rear of the Beetle (naturally!) and accessible from both inside and out. Note the two electric blowers, used to supply cooling air to the enclosed engine.

◀ Full steam ahead! Stewart opens the throttle wide and speeds across the water. Onlookers can't believe their eyes when the Waterbug comes into view. The realistic-looking wheels and tires are actually molded from fiberglass.

▲ The Waterbug is steered just like a car. The speed is controlled by a hand throttle, mounted between the seats where the gearshift would normally be on a Beetle. Gas tank is located by the driver's feet.

▼ Baja Bugs are essentially cut-down Beetles, designed for off-road use in the desert. However, this example looks like it spends more time climbing mountains and collecting trophies at auto shows! Who needs a four-by-four?

▶ The Meyers Tow'd was one of the first professionally-built off-road vehicles to be based on the Beetle, although all it relied on was the Beetle's suspension and driveline—the body and chassis were entirely new.

▶ The ultimate expression of an off-road VW is the sand rail. Built to climb the dunes at Glamis and Pismo Beach, California, sand rails are frequently powered by extremely powerful full-on race motors. Can anybody guess at its power-to-weight ratio?

▶ *Night time at Competition Hill, Glamis. Literally dozens, if not hundreds, of sand rails gather for a nocturnal blast up and down the slopes of this massive dune. It's truly a sight that has to be seen to be believed.*

▲ *What's a Golf doing in a book*
◀ *about the Bug? Well, perhaps everything isn't quite what it seems, for Bill Mathes' cabriolet is not your everyday water-cooled Volkswagen—and we're not just talking about its off-road styling! The secret lies around the back, for this Golf is powered by a rear-mounted, air-cooled engine, hooked up to a Beetle transmission! The owner uses the car for recreational trips down into Mexico and the Baja Peninsula.*

▶ While many off-roaders are clearly built solely for fun, others have a more serious purpose. This well-equipped Baja Bug is kitted out with water containers and heavy skid plates in readiness for the 1999 Africa Beetle Marathon.

▲ You don't want to worry about having to clean your Beetle? How about a back-to-basics Bug with hot rod styling? This fun machine was built on a shoe-string in France and received as much attention as a full-on show car!

▶ Most dune buggies are built for off-road fun or, at least, to give the appearance of being prepared for off-road use. However, there's a growing breed of Super Street Buggies—red-hot sportsters for the road.

▲ The caption on the back of this photograph reads "Florida—where else?". Wild-looking Baja is unlikely to win any beauty contests but looks like it's ready to take on allcomers out in the bush. Name on the door reads "Bad Apple II".

▼ Beauty is always said to be in the eye of the beholder, and clearly somebody loves this Bug enough to have spent many hours creating a wild custom. It may not be everyone's idea of perfection but, hey, it's different!

▲ Do you have a passion for racing Porsches but not the bottomless bank balance to enable you to indulge your fantasies? The Laser 917 could be the answer. Swoopy fiberglass kit car is based on a Beetle chassis.

◄ Or maybe you always fancied a vintage roadster from the 1930s? Again, if your fantasies aren't matched by your finances, a fiberglass kit car like this can provide miles of "classic" motoring for a fraction of the cost of the real thing.

▶ Is it a motorcycle? Is it a
▼ Volkswagen? Actually, it's both!
VW-powered trikes have been
around since the 1960s, and
combine the wind-in-the-hair
excitement of a motorcycle with the
reliability of a Beetle. This French-
built example is pure motorcycle at
the front, but looks like a cut-down
dune buggy from the back. Lots of
fun—when it isn't raining.

▶ Everybody
loves their
Bug—it's just
that some love
theirs more
than others!
This butterfly-
bedecked Bug
attracts a lot of
attention.
Hardly
surprising when
you check out
the "window
boxes" and
fence posts
along its side!

◀ Is air-
cooled, flat-four
power not
enough for
your tastes? The
answer could be
to build a
monster with a
V-8 in the front.
The chromed
and polished
motor looks
right at home
under the
hood of this
amazing Bug.

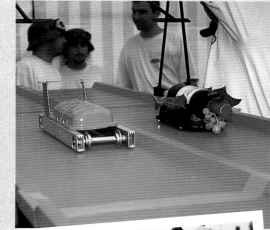

▲ Valve-cover racing has been around for years in V-8 circles and is now starting to gather momentum (no pun intended) among VW enthusiasts. All that's required is a gentle slope and plenty of imagination.

◄ There's nothing like starting them young! This VW enthusiast proudly wears her new T-shirt, bought for her at the last Volkswagen show. Is she asleep or simply dreaming of her first Bug? Now let's see— it's got to be pink, no, yellow...

▲ Part of the fun of restoring or customizing a Beetle is searching out the parts needed to finish your project. While some items can be bought new, others can only be found by rummaging around at swap meets.

► The world's most famous Volkswagen: Herbie the Love Bug! Immortalised by Disney, this VW with a heart of gold took on allcomers in the film "Herbie Goes To Monte Carlo". Photo copyright of Walt Disney Productions

Chapter 11

SPORTING BUGS

Zero to sixty in *how* long?

It's well documented that, immediately after the war, the Porsche family began to draw up designs for a VW-based sports car, the end result of which was the famous Porsche 356. However, the Porsches weren't the only people to take a close look at the VW for use in sporting applications.

Among the first to exploit the Volkswagen's potential was Petermax Müller, a future Volkswagen dealer in Germany. Müller built a number of relatively sophisticated, aluminum-bodied, single-seat racing cars which relied heavily on contemporary Volkswagen components, including the engine, front and rear suspension, wheels, and even the gas tank.

But not everyone saw the need to dispense with the traditional Beetle bodyshell to have some fun in motorsport. Rallying was always a popular sport, especially in Europe, with events such as the Monte Carlo Rally creating huge public interest. The Beetle acquitted itself well, and continues to do so today in historic rallying. The ruggedness of the design lends itself well to coping with the hardships of competing against the clock over long distances.

This ruggedness has also made this humble

A "Beetle" meets its maker at the hands of a stock-car driver in England in the 1950s. This form of racing was popular as it provided thrills without major expense. Sadly, it also saw the demise of many a collectible car.

car so popular in all kinds of off-road racing, from severe tests of endurance, such as the infamous Mexican Baja 1000, to the popular European sports of rallycross and autocross. Off-road racing, Baja-style, has seen the creation of breathtakingly engineered, pure-bred race cars. Raced to the edge of destruction, these VWs-on-steroids—with their long-travel suspension, heavy-duty chassis, and extensive safety equipment—seem capable of withstanding virtually any form of punishment.

The European sports of rallycross (held on a mixture of asphalt and dirt) and autocross have been the happy hunting ground of VW-based vehicles for many years. It was only with the appearance of four-wheel-drive machines, notably in the form of competition-prepared Audi quattros, that the Beetle finally had to accept second best—well, almost. Today, there are still some stalwarts who continue to carry a

torch for the Beetle, among them Englishman Peter Harrold, who, in the late 1990s, competed in a specially-built four-wheel-drive version.

Road racing is one form of sport in which skeptics may feel that the Beetle has no chance. However, in South America, enthusiasts have been racing Beetles for decades, while, in Europe, the Germans currently compete in the Käfer Cup and the French in the similar Super VW Cup. Highly modified cars feature large-capacity engines (often around 2.5 liters), Porsche gearboxes, and four-wheel disc brakes!

But the Beetle (or at least its components) also excels in another area of circuit racing, namely Formula Vee. This is a relatively low-cost formula for single-seat, open-wheeled cars powered by modified Beetle engines.

Unlikely as it may seem, when one considers the lowly power output, another area in which the Beetle excels is the macho sport of drag racing, where horsepower generally wins the day. As many owners of Detroit-built machines have found to their cost, the combination of a highly modified, air-cooled VW engine in a relatively light sedan can prove very effective!

Petermax Müller built this beautiful aluminum-bodied race car using the components from a late 1940s Beetle. It was capable of over 120 miles per hour and can be seen on display in the Volkswagen Museum at Wolfsburg.

▲ Built some time around 1960, this South American VW regularly competed in road races. It was essentially a Beetle that had been "sectioned" (a slice had been removed from all round the body).

▲ Beetles played a regular part in motorsport in the late 1950s and early 1960s. The Beetle seen here during a refueling stop was part of a "works" team run by Scania Vabis, the Swedish VW importer, and driven by rally legend Eric Carlsson.

◀ Miss World greets a competitor in the 1953 Monte Carlo Rally at a control point in Paris. Although a Beetle never actually won a Monte Carlo Rally, VWs competed regularly. Note the "bug deflector" mounted on the hood, in an effort to keep the windshield clean.

▶ A service stop for the works car of Bertil Söderström and R. Olsson on the 1964 RAC Rally in Great Britain. These cars were fitted with Okrasa-style engines and Porsche 356B brakes. Note the heavy stone guard under the sump.

▼ Rallycross was another popular European motorsport, notably in the 1970s and 1980s. For years Beetles were dominant, especially vehicles like Cees Teurlings' Super Beetle with its 200-plus horsepower engine and Porsche transmission.

▶ Not all motorsport is glamorous! What's known as "stock car racing" in Europe is a far cry from the current NASCAR stock car racing in the United States! What appears to be a VW is, in fact, an old Ford with a Beetle body (and an Oval at that!).

◀ Perhaps the ultimate rallycross Beetle was Peter Harrold's four-wheel-drive machine. It featured a turbocharged and fuel-injected flat-four VW engine equipped with water-cooled Subaru four-cam cylinder heads.

◀ In the United States, Volkswagens have always been the number-one choice for off-road racing, thanks largely to their robust construction and mechanical reliability. Cut-down Beetles such as this are generally referred to as "Baja Bugs".

▼ Taking things a stage further, this off-road race machine features a full tube-chassis clothed in replica Beetle bodywork. Long-travel suspension allows the vehicle to drive at speed over rough terrain without damage.

▶ Sand drag racing has also seen Volkswagen-powered machinery dominate. This dragster may not look much like a Beetle, but its turbocharged engine and transmission are derived from those fitted to the People's Car.

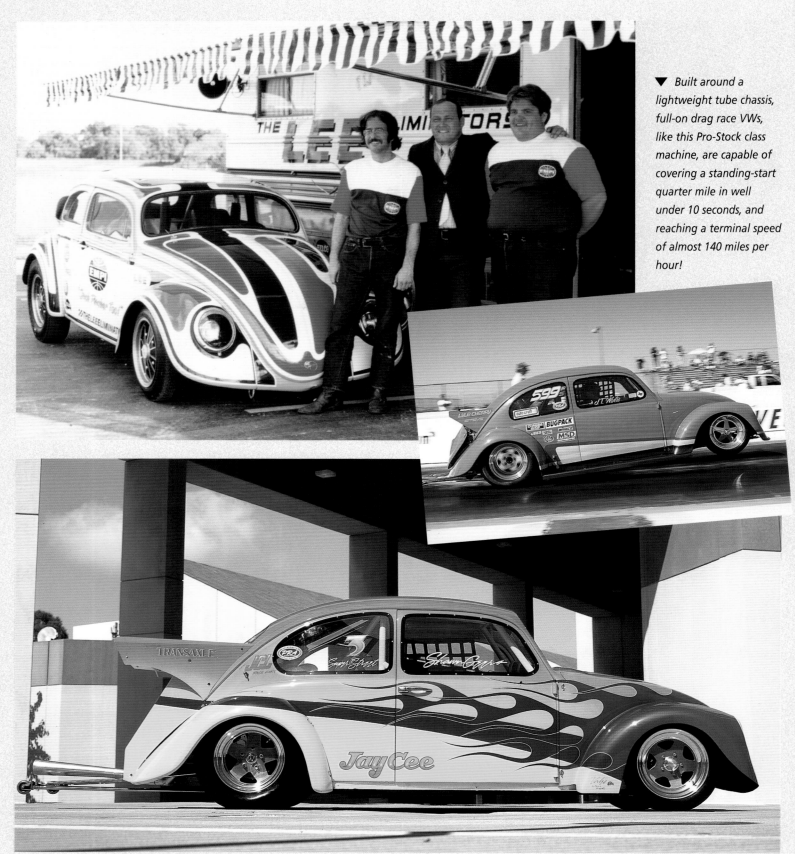

▶ Probably the most famous Volkswagen drag car of all time was EMPI's Inch Pincher, driven by Darrell Vittone (left). Volkswagens were front-runners in certain classes of national drag racing competition throughout the 1960s, regularly beating much more powerful rivals.

▶ Drag racing has always attracted show-quality vehicles, such as Sean Geers' Super-Street class Beetle. Although based on a stock VW floorpan, it's still capable of hitting close to 130 miles per hour at the end of the quarter mile.

▼ Built around a lightweight tube chassis, full-on drag race VWs, like this Pro-Stock class machine, are capable of covering a standing-start quarter mile in well under 10 seconds, and reaching a terminal speed of almost 140 miles per hour!

▲ Ken Fisher in Florida decided to do things differently by building a "roofless" Beetle with a tube chassis and mid-mounted engine, thus placing the driver out in front. The end result was an extremely aerodynamic machine.

▼ In the 1960s and early 1970s, there were many weird and not-so-wonderful Beetle creations on the drag strips of England, including this one powered by a Jaguar XK straight-six engine, run by Michael Sharpe. Beautiful is not the first word that springs to mind!

▲ In England, back in the 1960s, intrepid Dave LeCoq drag raced this amazing motorcycle called the "Drag-Waye". It was powered by a sideways-mounted, supercharged Beetle motor that drove the back wheel via a chain.

▶ What started out as Outrage, with a flat-four VW-style engine, developed into a V8-powered "Funny Car" called Eightrage! Keith Deal is the brave driver of this crowd-pleasing car, which vies for the title of the World's Fastest Beetle.

▲ Mike Shelden—known to all
◀ as "Muffler Mike"—always puts on a great show for the spectators. This sequence, shot at a drag strip at Whitman, Arizona, shows Mike's car, front wheels pawing the air, as it leaves the start line.

▲ Super VW Cup racing is very competitive and spectators can be guaranteed thrills aplenty as the Beetles jostle for position. Many rounds of the championship are held alongside other race series, hence the mix of cars seen here, at Paul Ricard in France.

◀ Formula Vee has been around since the 1960s and many great race drivers have started their careers in this category. Vees have modified 1300cc single-port VW engines, and must retain Beetle front suspension and stock gearboxes.

▲ Germany stages the Käfer Cup and France the Super VW Cup, both nationwide road-race series using highly-tuned Beetles with engines of up to 2.5 liters. Lap times are close to those set by race-modified Porsche 911s.

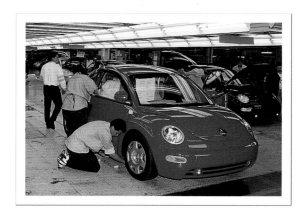

Chapter 12

THE NEW BEETLE

A car of the future—or a blast from the past?

When, in January 1994, the doors opened at the Detroit Auto Show, word had already spread that Volkswagen was going to unveil something rather special. For several years, the German company had been developing a "sub-compact"—called the Chico—as a stablemate to the European VW Polo, but nothing had been seen in public. In fact, some time earlier, the plug had been pulled on the project just as the car was, supposedly, about to go into production. Perhaps this was finally to be the Chico's finest hour?

As an expectant crowd of the world's motoring press gathered round the VW stand, few could have been prepared for the shock which awaited them. As staff threw back the covers obscuring the vehicle in the center of the stand, gasps of wonder—and delight—swept through the crowd. Nobody had expected this…

And just what caused the hardened press reporters to react so spontaneously? It was a small, bright yellow, rounded sedan which looked unsure whether it was coming or going. Immediately, parallels were drawn between this car and the original Beetle: its curved lines, the

The staff of Volkswagen in Mexico cares as much about quality control as their predecessors in Wolfsburg in the 1960s. Each completed vehicle is thoroughly checked for imperfections before delivery.

happy "face", the running boards, the horn grills, the headlights…It was as if the Beetle had been given a dose of the Elixir of Life.

Concept One, as the styling project was officially known, transformed VW's image overnight. Previously, the company had been regarded as deeply conservative, but it was now seen to be not only looking to the future, but also trying to put some fun back into motoring, at a time when conservationists appeared to be intent on forcing cars off the road.

Concept One was the brainchild of two designers at Volkswagen's secret design facility in Simi Valley, California. J.C. Mays and Freeman Thomas trained at the American Art Center College of Design. From there, they moved to Germany, Thomas joining Porsche in Stuttgart, Mays working with Audi at Ingolstadt. In 1991, they returned to the United States to open the American Design Center for Audi and VW.

What makes the Concept One unusual (apart from its styling!) is the fact that the design was drawn up without a brief from Volkswagen in Germany. It was very much the product of the imagination of the two young designers who, realizing that small cars were generally considered to be unexciting, felt it was time to put some pizzazz back into motoring.

Concept One certainly attracted a huge amount of media attention at Detroit, its image being broadcast round the world within hours, much to VW's delight. However, what nobody quite expected was the immediate outcry from VW dealers across the United States who became besieged with potential customers all demanding to know when and where they could buy this "new Bug".

Just as the world's press was thinking the bright yellow prototype (in reality, it was more of a styling mock-up than working prototype) was the end of the story, Volkswagen came back with a second attack on convention: a Concept One cabriolet. First shown at the 1994 Geneva Motor Show in Switzerland, the bright red, open-topped Concept was another showstopper. Volkswagen was clearly taking this project very seriously and the public demand increased to such an extent that Volkswagen of America even published a toll-free number so that enthusiasts could register their interest.

Initially, whenever the topic of production came up in conversation, Volkswagen hinted that, if Concept One did make it into the showroom, it would be based on the chassis and front-wheel-drive layout of the existing Polo model. As far as cost was concerned, again there were hints that its price would be similar to that of the Polo—VW's least expensive car.

Conceived as a car for the future, Concept One broke new ground in terms of its driveline. Volkswagen engineers envisaged the car being powered by a variety of engines, including a technically fascinating "hybrid" unit, which combined a turbocharged diesel with an 18kW electric motor.

However, reality proved to be something rather different, for the third prototype design, shown in Japan in 1995, was based on the driveline of the larger VW Golf. On the positive side, this opened up all kinds of possibilities for engine selection, including the acclaimed narrow-angle VR6 unit used in the top-of-the-range Golf, Jetta, and Passat models. On the negative side, the projected price had risen dramatically.

The most exciting news to break in Japan was that, yes, Volkswagen was going to build the car. Reaction from press and public alike had finally persuaded Volkswagen to give the project the go-ahead, although it was unlikely to be in production much before the end of the Millennium.

VW held one other ace up its sleeve. In 1996, news broke that the car would no longer be referred to as Concept One—its official title would be the "New Beetle"! Production was now destined to begin some time in 1997, (although, this proved too optimistic—the first New Beetles didn't appear in U.S. dealerships until early in 1998). The Volkswagen publicity machine moved into top gear: a website was set up on the Internet, and a whole range of merchandising made available for impatient enthusiasts who could not wait another year to drive their own piece of history. The New Beetle promised to be a sales success before it even turned a wheel.

When the car was eventually launched, initially only in North America, VW dealers reported lines of people anxious to place a deposit on a car they hadn't even seen, let alone driven. Never before had there been such hysteria over a car which nobody could yet own—except, maybe, back in 1938 when Adolf Hitler spoke about the People's Car in Berlin!

When deliveries did begin to arrive at the showrooms, there were tales of rival customers entering into "bidding wars", each offering the dealer more money in an effort to purchase one of the first examples. Even a year later, New Beetles were frequently being offered for sale at more than the sticker price—this in an age when most new cars are discounted in an effort to sell them quickly. The New Beetle was clearly perceived to be something rather special.

But perhaps the most surprising twist to the tale was that the New Beetle wasn't even built in Wolfsburg—or anywhere else in Germany, for that matter. No, Herbie's new cousin (the New Beetle is too far removed from Porsche's original design to be called a brother!) is built in Mexico, alongside the air-cooled original, at Volkswagen's modern Puebla factory.

As far as the Mexican plant is concerned, the decision to move production to Puebla is the greatest compliment that could be paid to the workers and management, for the New Beetle is one of the most important vehicles in VW's history. It may not be the most expensive car in the range, but it's the one that has attracted most attention, and many rivals have been only too keen to find fault with build quality.

The story of Beetle production began over 60 years earlier, in a wooden workshop alongside Porsche's home in Stuttgart, and looks set to end thousands of miles away. It's unlikely that a Beetle will ever be built again in Germany. However, one thing is for sure: there's currently no end in sight, wherever it's built. The original Beetle was the car of 20th century—the New Beetle looks set to be the car of the 21st.

The covers come off the New Beetle—well, a clay mock-up, at least. Nobody was quite ready for the incredible public interest in this amazing new Volkswagen. Even the dealers were caught by surprise by the rush of people.

▼ From the outset, in 1992, the Concept One project was conceived as a way to put some fun back into motoring—this humorous sketch depicts Volkswagen's new baby as a toy, pulled along by a piece of string!

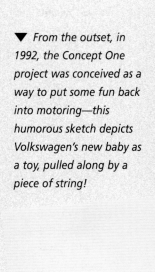

◄ Early drawings
▼ explored the idea of an automobile that was heavily influenced by the original People's Car. The rounded side windows and louvers under the rear window are clear references to Porsche's design. One idea was to make the front and rear fenders interchangeable, not only to lower manufacturing costs but also to reduce the quantity of stock held by dealerships—sadly, this didn't make it past the drawing board.

◀ *As the project gathered momentum, Freeman Thomas who, with J. C. Mays, came up with the Concept One idea, made several detailed sketches to explore the idea of a "retro" Volkswagen. Note the round door mirrors on this design.*

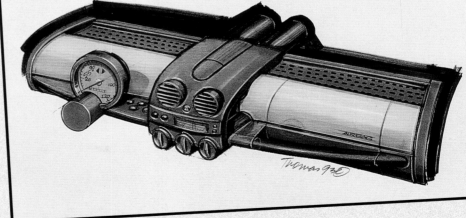

◀ *Steering wheel design is a vital element in a vehicle's character—after all, it's what the driver sees most while driving. Several possibilities are shown here, all with a retro feel. Note, too, the Concept One ignition key!*

▲ *Concept One's dashboard was given a very distinctive look—part retro, part futuristic. The single instrument (a round speedometer) and passenger grab handle were intended to remind occupants of the original Beetle.*

◀ Once Thomas and Mays were happy with the way the Concept One project was progressing, the next step was to build a ¼-scale model. This allowed the designers to view their new baby from all angles. Note the dummy horn grilles in the front fenders.

▼ Another model showing a different approach to the front-end styling. Compared with the earlier design, the front has been made wider, the dummy horn grilles moved outwards, and the wheels altered.

▶ The model still retained round door mirrors and louvers under the rear window—sadly, these features weren't carried over to production cars. Front and rear fenders were still envisaged as being interchangeable.

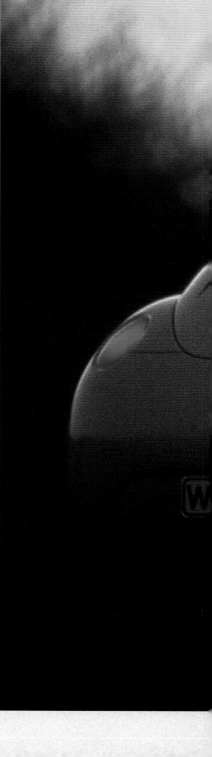

▼ Once the project had been given the go-ahead by Ferdinand Piëch, head of Volkswagen, a full-size, electric-powered styling exercise was built for the January 1994 Detroit Auto Show. The response was overwhelming, from press and public alike.

▶ Following the showing of the two Concept One design studies, Volkswagen came under great pressure from dealers in North America to put the car into production. To do so would require a lot of work on the part of the in-house designers.

▶ Two months later, at Geneva, Volkswagen stole the headlines again with this stunning cabriolet version of the Concept One design. It was at this point that people realized Volkswagen was deadly serious about building such a car.

One of the first decisions was to increase the car's wheelbase so that it would be possible to accommodate the drivetrain and still allow adequate interior space for four adults. The stylized running boards echo those of the original Beetle.

▲ If Concept One was to be put
▶ into production, serious thought had to be given to practical matters, such as lighting and crash protection. The front end was redesigned to accommodate bumpers and turn signals. At the rear, the mock louvers disappeared from beneath the window, and consideration was given to license plate mountings and a high-level brake light. However, the design lost little of its original appeal.

◀ The next step in the process of making the car production-ready was to create full-size drawings and a clay model, so that every aspect of the appearance could be examined in detail.

▲ This full-size drawing shows how relatively little the final version of the car changed from that first Concept One show car seen at Detroit. By now, the decision had been made to base the car on the platform of the VW Golf Mk4 and Audi A3.

▶ Although this photo shows a promotional mock-up, producing a proper full-size clay model is a long-winded process. It requires the creation of a wooden buck that is then covered in modeling clay, ready for the stylists to get to work.

◀ One of the advantages of producing a clay mock-up is that different design details can be tried out alongside each other. Here, for example, two headlight designs are under consideration. Clay modeling is a highly-skilled occupation.

▶ Once the clay model is completed, reference lines are laid across it to enable the shape to be traced by computer. In this way, it's then possible to go ahead and produce the tooling necessary to create prototype body panels.

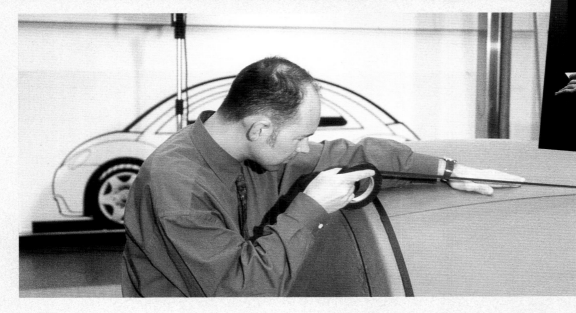

▲ With all the co-ordinates entered into the computer, the designer can create a three-dimensional image on screen. This cuts out much of the time-consuming engineering drawing traditionally required.

▶ In October 1995, VW displayed this restyled version of the Concept One at the Tokyo Motor Show, where it was announced that the car would be called the New Beetle. This was followed five months later by the European launch at the 1996 Geneva Motor Show.

▼ The Geneva show car (seen here) featured a full-length opening glass sunroof—yet another clever idea that never made it past the prototype stage. However, the overall design had been more or less finalized by this stage.

◀ It was decided that the New Beetle would be built at the Puebla plant in Mexico, home of "original" Beetle production in South America. The butterfly-roofed entrance facility still looks the same as when it was built in the 1950s.

▼ Staff and management at the Mexican plant are proud of being given the task of assembling the New Beetle. Everywhere around the factory there are signs displaying the stylish New Beetle logo.

◀ The assembly lines are spotlessly clean—a far cry from the production lines at Wolfsburg in the 1940s. Here, bare bodyshells are being fitted with rubber tailgate seals and interior sound-deadening trim.

▶ Carried on overhead lines, these bodyshells are being fitted with the rear suspension sub-assembly. Note that the electrical wiring harness and headliner have already been installed further back down the line.

▲ Engine and transmission are assembled on their own lines, and then fitted as one package. The New Beetle uses essentially the same driveline as that fitted to the Mk4 Golf—a tried and tested combination.

◀ This photo shows the driveline and front suspension assembly being fitted to a New Beetle. Modern assembly-line technology allows much of the work to be carried out by no more than two people at a time.

▲ A complete dashboard sub-assembly ready for installation in a car. The original design intent, with a prominent, retro-styled speedometer directly ahead of the driver, was preserved for production.

Ouch! A New Beetle undergoes a side-impact test. Distressing though this may be to a Volkswagen enthusiast, every new model has to be tested literally to destruction to establish its ability to withstand a major collision.

Old meets new: a Mexican-built, air-cooled Beetle drives past a line of completed New Beetles awaiting delivery to the United States. Will the New Beetle last to the end of the new century? Only time will tell.

▲ Robotized parts delivery! This little motorized cart follows the lines painted on the floor, delivering components—in this case a new fender—to a pre-programmed destination. This saves time and, ultimately, money.

Chapter 13

THE NEW WAVE

Even the New Beetle gets the custom treatment

It seemed that, no sooner had the New Beetle been launched, than people began to seek out ways to make them more individual—despite there being a waiting list which, in some instances, stretched over several months. For some reason, the desire to be different was as strong among New Beetle owners as it ever had been among enthusiasts of the original air-cooled design!

The first two (privately imported) cars to arrive in Britain, for example, were almost immediately transformed, with lowered suspension and aftermarket wheels—one even being turned into a Herbie "Love Bug" look-alike with carefully applied vinyl graphics!

There have been many other references to the Beetle's past, with one German company offering a fake split-window conversion aimed to make the New Beetle take on the appearance of the pre-1954 models. Kamei, long-established German manufacturer of accessories for Volkswagens, even produced retro-styled gravel guards to fit the rear fenders of the new model, mimicking those fitted in the 1950s and 1960s to old Beetles.

No sooner had the New Beetle been put into production than a German company offered a fake split-window kit. The idea was to make the car look like the early Beetles—all it takes is imagination (and a few beers!).

But there are some people who prefer to regard the New Beetle as a thoroughly modern car and treat it accordingly. By following the current trend for fitting large-diameter (up to 19-inch) aluminum wheels and low profile tires to cars that have been radically lowered, the whole character of the New Beetle can be changed in an instant.

That owners would wish to pursue this style of customizing is, perhaps, somewhat predictable, as it's very much in vogue—less so is the desire among some to use shock tactics to gain attention! What possesses a person to air-brush graveyard scenes and mold skulls over their brand new car? Come to that, how about carrying around a 400-pound imitation lobster on the roof of your New Beetle? That's what a seafood restaurant in Boston does to create publicity—and it works!

Even Volkswagen got in on the act by

creating a series of "art cars" as a result of a competition held over the Internet to design a paint scheme which reflected the fun character of the New Beetle.

Literally thousands of entries were received, the winning designs being transferred by highly-skilled air-brush artists onto a range of New Beetles. These cars were then displayed around Germany before finally being put on show at the Volkswagen Museum in Wolfsburg.

To further promote the New Beetle as something rather special, Volkswagen has backed a race series—the New Beetle Cup—which features highly modified cars competing on a number of race tracks throughout Germany. There have also been privately-built drag racing New Beetles, including examples in the United States (California, where else?) powered by rear-mounted, air-cooled engines. Now that's turning full circle.

So, it seems that no matter how hard you try, you can't get away from the original concept—ask any enthusiast where the engine is on a REAL Beetle and the answer will always be the same: at the back, where it belongs!

◀ Richard Straman in Huntington Beach, California, was among the first to build what everybody was really waiting for: a New Beetle cabriolet. With its electric-powered top, the Straman convertible is a very attractive car.

▲ Driving a New Beetle al fresco is a whole new experience! Thanks to substantial strengthening, the bodyshell remains equally as rigid (if not more so) than the original hardtop. It's just perfect for the California sunshine.

▲ There's a price to pay for such a conversion—New Beetle roof sections lined up outside the Straman workshop. They won't be sent for scrap, though, for there's a demand for such panels within the accident repair trade.

▶ You'll never "tire" of driving this New Beetle. French tire manufacturer Michelin showed this interpretation at the Detroit Auto Show in 1999—is this the ultimate customized New Beetle?

▲ Don't look now, but there's a lobster following you! This crazy conversion was carried out to promote a chain of seafood restaurants in the United States. With the lobster weighing some 400 pounds, one can only imagine what the handling is like.

▶ Everybody went World Cup crazy in 1998, including the owner of this New Beetle spotted in Illinois! The rounded lines of the New Beetle lend themselves well to the transformation from Bug to soccer ball.

◀ If the stock New Beetle isn't big enough for you, then maybe this inflatable version is what you need. Used to promote the New Beetle Cup race series in Germany, it's the ideal car for the expanding family. Need more room? Just pump it up!

▼ Volkswagen is heavily into sponsoring rock bands and musicians, including the legendary guitarist Eric Clapton. He has his own New Beetle, but is seen here posing with one of the cars from the Art Tour in Germany.

▲ Volkswagen
▶ held a
competition over the
internet, asking
people to design a
paint scheme for the
New Beetle. The
winning designs—
here are "flower
power" and leopard
themes—were then
air-brushed onto
New Beetles for
display across
Germany. Can you
guess at the repair
bill if somebody
scratched one.

◀ Gary Uroegh's New Beetle from Arizona got the hot-rod treatment courtesy of these wild flames applied over the original Techno Blue paint. Curved body panels of the New Beetle are perfect for flame paint jobs.

▼ This "roped-and-tied" New Beetle formed part of the celebrations in the Weimar region of Germany in 1999. As one of the main sponsors of "Weimar 1999—European Capital of Culture", Volkswagen provided the organisers with a fleet of 25 cars.

▶ "Bugzilla" is the name of this breathtaking New Beetle painted by Toni Carlini from California (where else?). The blend of leopard spots and flames is unusual, to say the least, but the overall effect is simply stunning.

153

▶ The New Beetle soon captured the imagination of the aftermarket industry. Autobahn Designs, of Riverside, California, lowered this New Beetle then added some 18-inch wheels and a subtle body kit to create a stylish, Porsche-like custom.

▶ Volkswagen soon got in on the act, too. At the 1999 Detroit Auto Show, the VW display centered round this aggressive-looking styling exercise called the New Beetle RSi. Huge rear spoiler changed the whole character of the car!

▲ The RSi's interior was amazing, as the dashboard featured plenty of billet aluminum and carbon-fiber detailing. Check out that wild-looking gear shift! The design of the RSi was clearly influenced by race-car engineering.

▶ This may look like another New Beetle that has simply been lowered and fitted with aftermarket wheels and low-profile tires, but appearances can be deceptive. Certainly the exterior gives away few clues as to what lies under the hood.

▲ Not content with a modest 2-litèr, four-cylinder stocker, HPA Motorsports
◀ in the United States installed one of Volkswagen's superb 2.8-liter VR6 motors—a complex task that's definitely not for the faint-hearted. With over 200 horsepower on tap, this New Beetle enjoys life in the fast lane.

▶ For some people, the New Beetle's interior is just a little too conservative. Little John's Interior Concepts in Fountain Valley, California, was responsible for this show-stopping upholstery featured in the leopard-flamed "Bugzilla".

▲ For a more subtle look, Gary Uroegh had his local upholstery shop retrim the seats of his New Beetle to include the famous VW logo in relief. Leather was then used to add some contrasting trim panels on the stock seats.

▲ We couldn't resist showing this twosome—a New Beetle being used to tow a 1967 "original" Beetle. That's what we call keeping it in the family.

▲ The prize for the
◄ most weird New
Beetle of all must go to
Leo Ceballos of Miami
Beach, Florida. An air-
brush artist called
"Daytona Flash" was
responsible for the
outrageous paintwork of
this "Krypt Keeper" show
car. Even the interior was
given the full treatment,
with ghoulish three-
dimensional skulls molded
into the door panels and
stone-effect artwork air-
brushed over the tweed
interior trim. Not a car for
the squeamish.

▲ Everyone involved with building this New Beetle at VW's Mexican factory signed the bodywork before the car was shipped to Germany for display in the Volkswagen Museum at Wolfsburg.

◀ The owners of these two New Beetles preferred to give their cars a touch of individuality in a more restrained fashion: personalized license plates sum up their feelings for their cars.

◄ The New Beetle Cup race series in Germany led to the development of a new breed of New Beetle, powered by a 2.8-liter, 200-horsepower VR6 engine with a six-speed gearbox. The cars also feature 18-inch light-alloy wheels and slick tires.

▼ The New Beetle Cup is very close and competitive, with full fields of similarly powered cars providing entertaining racing for the crowds. New Beetles have also been in action in ice racing and drag racing, among other motorsports.

INDEX